J. C. G. George, FSA (Scot)
Garioch Pursuivant of Arms

The Puffin Book of
FLAGS

Illustrated by Raymond Turvey

Puffin Books

Puffin Books, Penguin Books Ltd, Harmondsworth,
Middlesex, England
Penguin Books, 625 Madison Avenue,
New York, New York 10022, U.S.A.
Penguin Books Australia Ltd, Ringwood,
Victoria, Australia
Penguin Books Canada Ltd, 2801 John Street,
Markham, Ontario, Canada L3R 1B4
Penguin Books (N.Z.) Ltd, 182–190 Wairau Road,
Auckland 10, New Zealand

First published by Puffin Books 1978
Published simultanously in hardcover by Kestrel Books

Text copyright © J. C. G. George, 1978
Illustrations copyright © Raymond Turvey, 1978
All rights reserved

Made and printed in Great Britain by
Richard Clay (The Chaucer Press) Ltd,
Bungay, Suffolk
Set in Monotype Ehrhardt

Contents

To the greater glory of Almighty God
to whom all nations owe allegiance
this book is humbly and gratefully dedicated

Acknowledgements

To my darling wife, Margaret, who, in a very busy life, lovingly
gave her precious time to type every word in this book, I extend
my deepest gratitude. I also thank Mr D. S. Quinn who read
and checked the proofs, Raymond Turvey who has provided
such excellent illustrations, Dorothy Wood my editor, Marilyn
Taylor her assistant, Andrew Best and Frances Kelly of Curtis
Brown Academic Ltd and the staffs of the British Library and
the Old Brompton Road branch of the Chelsea and Kensington
Library, and the Council of The Heraldry Society for all the
advice and help which they have given unsparingly.

Author's Note

All the information in this book is correct at the time of going
to press. However, things change all the time, and it may well
be that by the time the book is published new countries will
have emerged and others may have changed their flags. For any
such errors and omissions we can only ask the reader's
indulgence.

FLAGS

The men of Israel shall camp
by their troops, ensigns and standards.

Holy Bible, Numbers ii, 2.

The Book of Numbers, from which this quotation is taken, records the events which took place during the period in which Moses lived, usually thought to be about the year 1400 BC. Even then flags were obviously not a new invention because the quotation suggests that some system of distinguishing one ensign and standard (which in many ways is only another word for a flag or an object of the same nature and purpose as a flag) from another had not only already been worked out but was also understood and recognized by the ordinary people living at the time.

Nor was it only in the Bible lands of Egypt and Israel that flags were used so early. In the year 1122 BC an old Chinese scribe wrote that whenever the then ruler, Emperor Chou, went out in a formal procession he always had a white flag carried before him.

There is also evidence that the ancient Greeks, from about the beginning of the fourth century BC, and probably even earlier, used to raise a purple cloth on a spear or lance as the signal for the army to advance. It is believed to have been called a *phoinikis* (pronounced foi*nee*kis), which, translated literally, is 'purple garment', so it was probably somebody's cloak or tunic. And Captain Barraclough in his book *Flags of the World* tells how Themistocles, the Admiral of the Greek navy, gave the signal to attack the Persian fleet at the battle of Salamis (480 BC) by ordering a red cloak to be tied to an oar and waved aloft.

The exact origin of the word flag is not known for certain, but it is believed to be derived from an old Saxon word *hleogan*, meaning to float in the wind which is, of course, just what flags do.

9

Like mankind, flags have evolved with the passing of the centuries. There are, and have been, many types of flags. Usually they have been designed for some particular purpose. Many of them have long been forgotten and are not usually seen nowadays because the need for which they were made no longer exists. Still, some of these were very beautiful and had fascinating stories attached to them so I have included a few of them in this book.

Their Purpose

Put up a flag and a person, a group or a place may be identified or recognized quickly by many people. In essence a flag is a pictorial representation of a name. Whereas, in Britain, we can read words written in the roman alphabet, most of us cannot read words written in, say, Cyrillic letters, the alphabet used in eastern Europe. But colours look and mean the same to everybody in the world; so do shapes, such as crosses, stars, stripes, lions, eagles, squares, triangles and many more.

What a Flag Means

Flags are the visible and tangible expression of a country's traditions, history and way of life. A country's flag embodies the whole spirit of a nation, which is why the sight of them arouses feelings either of pride or of enmity.

Consequently, the flag becomes a target when people or nations disagree with each other, and the capture and possible destruction of the enemy's flag is very important.

People always treat a flag with great respect. When an important one is carried in a ceremonial procession you will see that people in uniform salute it as it goes by, while civilians may stand still and, if they are wearing them, raise their hats or caps.

For example, in the United States of America there are strict regulations concerning the use of the Stars and Stripes and how it is to be disposed of when it has grown too old for further use.

The flag has always been regarded as very precious. In fact, during Napoleon's disastrous retreat from Moscow in 1812, the officers of the French Army, who had been entrusted with the care of the flags, burnt them and drank the ashes in melted snow to prevent them falling into the hands of the enemy.

The Composition and Parts
of a Flag

Nowadays flags are normally woven of a mixture of nylon and bunting, which is a coarse woollen cloth. The weave is traditionally a *breadth* of 22·8 cm (9 ins.) so a flag measuring 91·44 cm (3 ft) across would be said to be a flag of 'four breadths'.

Some flags, normally those of private individuals, which usually only fly indoors or in positions where they are not greatly exposed to the weather, are attached to their staffs by a *sleeve* sewn to the *hoist* of the flag.

Most flags have short ropes sewn on to them, ending just above the flag and trailing about 25–30 cm (10 to 12 ins.) below. The top end has a piece of wood called a *toggle* fixed into it while the lower end of the rope finishes in a loop. The toggle of the flag fits into a loop on the *halyards*, while the halyards' toggle fits into the loop of the flag rope. The halyards are the ropes fixed to the flag staff used for hauling the flag up and down. The loops into which the toggles fit are also called *beckets*.

The toggle and becket on a flag makes it almost impossible for it to be flown upside down by mistake. (See 'Flags as Distress Signals', on p. 15.)

An alternative to the loop and toggle arrangement is a device called an *Inglefield clip*, which is often used by the navy.

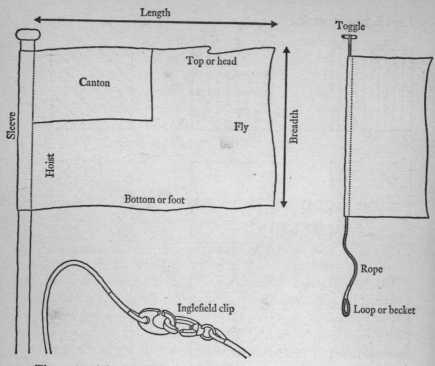

The parts of the flag

How to Tell the Colours

It is not possible to show all the flags pictured in this book in full colour, but there is a way of telling what colours the various parts of any particular flag are.

This system of indicating the various colours is not a new one, and has long been used in heraldry. It was invented by a man called Petra Sancta in 1638. The method is simple: all you have to look at is the type of shading. This will tell you what colour is being represented.

Here is how it works:

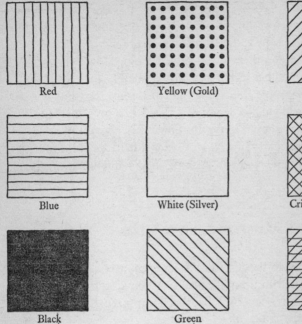

Red	Yellow (Gold)	Purple
Blue	White (Silver)	Crimson (Maroon)
Black	Green	Orange

Flag Usage

'Brailing'
(the flag)

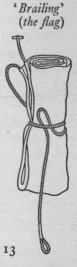

There are two ways of hoisting a flag. The first is by fixing the toggles and beckets and hauling it, flying in the breeze, all the way up, or by furling the flag into a neat bundle, with its ropes coiled round it in a certain way. This is called 'brailing' the flag. When a brailed flag is hoisted to the top of the staff, a sharp tug on the halyards releases the coiled ropes and the flag is then said to 'break' out.

Normally flags are hoisted at sunrise and lowered at sunset.

13

When a flag is lowered it should always be done in a slow and dignified way.

Saluting with flags is done by 'dipping', that is by slowly lowering and then re-hoisting the flag in one continuous action. Ships dip the ensign – the flag flown at the stern of the boat – when passing each other.

Flags are sometimes seen flying at 'half mast' – that is only half-way up the flag pole. This is a sign of mourning, and is used practically worldwide to denote the death of a great person.

National flags should never be flown one above the other, as this is a sign of victory in war. If, during a battle, a side lowers its flag completely this is called 'striking its colours' and is a sign of surrender.

Flags as Victory Signals

In wartime – in sea battles, too – when a country's flag is lowered and another one run up in its place, or above it, this means that the town or ship concerned has been captured by the country whose flag is flying on top.

During the war of 1812, when Britain was fighting America, one of the American ships surrendered to a British one. It signalled this by lowering its flag. A British crew was sent aboard the American ship to take it over and, to show that the ship was now in British hands, the officer in charge of the boarding party ran up two flags. Unfortunately he made a mistake! Instead of hoisting the Union Jack *over* the Stars and Stripes he put the Stars and Stripes *above* the Union Jack. When the captain of the British ship saw this he thought the Americans had captured the British boarding party, and again opened fire, killing most of the British boarding party, including the officer who had made the mistake. However, the American crew did not take advantage of this. They signalled the true state of affairs and honourably stood by their intention to surrender, and handed over their ship to a new British boarding party.

Flags as Distress Signals

The most usual way of using a flag to signal distress is to fly it upside down.

But as many flags look exactly, or nearly, the same upside down as they do the right way up, an alternative way is to tie a knot in it. This is sometimes called 'wefting' and looks like this:

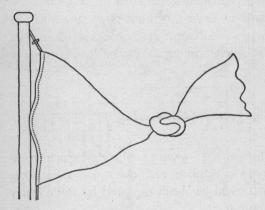

Very Early Flags and Standards

It is not known in detail what the earliest flags and standards were like but excavations by archaeologists indicate that things similar to what we think of as standards or flags were certainly in use from very early times.

THE EGYPTIANS

The armies of the Pharaohs used various emblems, believed to have been of a semi-sacred nature, fixed to the top of poles. These differed from regiment to regiment and included representations of sacred birds, effigies and other objects.

Very early flags and standards. Left to right: (1) Egyptian, (2) Assyrian, (3) Persian, (4) Greek, (5) Chinese

THE ASSYRIANS

The Assyrians were a very martial race and are known to have used a pole or staff topped by various emblems as standards. An example is illustrated.

THE PERSIANS

The Persians usually carried an eagle at the end of a spear, and also a representation of the sun depicted on a piece of cloth at the head of a staff.

THE GREEKS

The ancient Greeks placed a piece of armour, probably a breast-plate, on the top of a lance. Later on the various cities had their own emblems; for instance, Corinth used a Pegasus (a winged horse), Thebes a sphinx, and Athens an owl.

As already mentioned, the 'flag' used by the Athenian navy is believed to have been the purple tunic or cloak called the *phoinikis*.

THE CHINESE

As well as the white flag, which used to be carried before the Emperor Chou (see p.9), the Chinese almost certainly had many other flags. The most usual emblem which featured on them was a dragon; others carried simple arrangements of stripes.

The Roman Empire

The beginnings of some form of order and control of the use of flags and standards began to emerge in the days of ancient Rome. Just as modern armies consist of larger formations, such as divisions, broken down into brigades, battalions, companies and platoons, so the Roman Army was made up of legions subdivided into 'cohorts', 'centuries' and 'maniples'. The standard of the maniple (a group normally consisting of about fifty men) was often a handful of hay fixed to a staff. That of the cohort was usually either a dragon or a serpent.

The standard of the legion was, in early times, very varied. It was often a silver hand surrounded by a wreath placed on top of a spear, with a number of discs below on which were a variety of designs. Other legions might use animals and birds such as a wolf, bear, horse or eagle as their symbol. But over the years it became customary for a legion's standard to be the well-known eagle, which, in a slightly different form, was later adopted by Napoleon for the troops of imperial France.

The first flags recognizable as such and known to the western world were used by the Roman army. They were the *vexillum* and the *labarum*.

Left to right:
Roman eagle standard, the vexillum, the labarum

THE VEXILLUM

This was usually a square-shaped piece of richly fringed cloth hanging from a small crossbar fastened to the top of a staff. It was used principally by the Roman cavalry units so that they could recognize each other by the colour used and the design, if any, on the material. Because of the way the *vexillum* hung it is generally considered to be the forerunner of the gonfannon (see p. 27).

THE LABARUM

This was the imperial banner of the later Roman emperors. It was made of purple silk richly embroidered with the emperor's head or some other chosen device. The most notable of these was the ☧ symbol for Christ used by Constantine the Great. Sometimes the *labarum* was carried suspended from a crossbar like the *vexillum* and at other times it was flown in the same way as flags are today.

The Dark Ages

With the collapse of the Roman Empire in 476 western Europe was plunged into a long period of chaos and it seems there was little further advance in the development of flags until the advent of the Raven Flag in the ninth century.

The Raven Flag

This was the Vikings' flag. There do not appear to be any factual descriptions of it, but illustrations have been found on early English coins of the ninth century. It is shown like this.

The Raven Flag could have been the first flag to fly in America, as Ericson may have taken it with him on his famous journey in about the year 1000.

It is thought the Vikings used the raven emblem because its movement as the flag waved in the breeze was symbolic of victory.

The Battle of Hastings

By 1066 it seems that the use of flags and standards had become quite common practice. A lot can be seen on the famous Bayeux tapestry, which tells the story of this battle in picture form.

It shows King Harold standing by his serpent, or dragon, standard, and the square, three-tailed flag (sometimes called a gonfannon) with a cross between four roundels which had been blessed and given by the Pope to William the Conqueror.

Although organized heraldry was not yet known, its seeds can be clearly seen in these Hastings flags.

The Middle Ages

The Middle Ages saw the advent of organized heraldry, between 1100 and 1300. Heraldry is the means whereby individual people, groups and nations can be identified by the way the colours and symbols they use in flags, shields and so on, are arranged. Since the twelfth century, it has been subject to certain strict rules which are regulated by the heralds or appropriate authorities of each country.

In those days flags were primarily the emblems of kings and the nobility, and consequently they came to be treated with respect.

Flags were enormously important in any battle, which is why the fighting round them was always heaviest. The fall or capture of the flag so disheartened their followers that it was usually followed by defeat. They were always entrusted to the bravest officers, men who would give their lives before allowing the flag to be captured.

During the twelfth and thirteenth centuries battle flags became very large because they indicated the main rallying points of the army, and when there were big groups of men moving about the fighting area it was essential that these rallying points could be seen from a distance – they were usually the main places, or strategic spots, where the king and the commanders of the armies concerned had taken up their positions. The largest flags were too big for one man to carry so they were mounted on specially made wheeled platforms so that they could be moved from place to place.

An idea of just how important and big the battle flags of the twelfth and thirteenth centuries could be is given by the Battle of the Standard, which took place against the Scots in 1138.

The staff of the English 'standard' was the mast of a ship. It was set up on a large four-wheeled platform. At its top was a crucifix and a silver box, called a pyx, containing a Eucharist wafer. Hung round the mast were the flags of St John of Beverly, St Wilfred and St Peter.

As the Scots approached, the Bishop of Durham placed himself at the foot of the standard and read a prayer of absolution, with the whole English army kneeling before him.

When the Scots attacked the fiercest fighting was around the standard. Eventually the Scots were beaten off and 12,000 of their men were killed.

THE BATTLE OF AGINCOURT

The flags of armies drawn up before a battle in medieval times must have created a magnificent spectacle. Normally there would have been at least one flag for every hundred men.

At Agincourt, the sight of the French army must have been almost incredible if they used all the flags they were entitled to, for according to some accounts, among their dead alone were seven princes of the blood, one marshal, three dukes, thirteen counts, ninety-two barons, 1,500 knights and 8,000 gentlemen, all of whom would have been entitled to a flag of one sort or another. A total of nearly 10,000. One hundred and twenty-six French banners fell that day, leaving aside the many pennons, bannerets, guidons and standards.

On the English side there were only about thirty fatalities, of whom all but four – at the most – would have been entitled to use a flag.

King Henry V's order to start the battle was quite simply 'Banners advance', which further emphasizes the importance of flags.

Various Types of Flags

BANNER

Banners are normally heraldic in appearance and are usually the flag of a prominent person, a family or a group. They can be seen flying over large private houses, town halls and schools, for instance. When a distinguished man or the head of a large organization is travelling to an important function he sometimes flies a reduced version of his banner on his motor car.

STANDARD

This term is now used to denote the banner of a sovereign or a head of state – for example, 'the Royal Standard' flying over Buckingham Palace. But this type of flag is really a banner.

Strictly speaking a standard is a long thin flag with a tapering or rounded end which is sometimes swallow-tailed. Early British standards had either the cross of St George or St Andrew in the hoist depending on the nationality of their owners. Nowadays it has the owner's coat of arms. On the fly are his various emblems, such as the family crest, badge and motto. The colours of the fly are the person's 'livery' or family colours.

True standards are very rarely seen in England today. They are more common in Scotland where they are used by clan chiefs at Highland gatherings.

The length of a standard depends upon the owner's rank. Henry VIII laid down that a duke's should be seven yards long, an earl's six, a baron's five and a knight's four.

PENNON or PENNANT

This is a small triangular flag flown from a lance head. It can bear the owner's arms or one of his personal emblems. It often ended in two points like a swallow's tail. When a knight had been

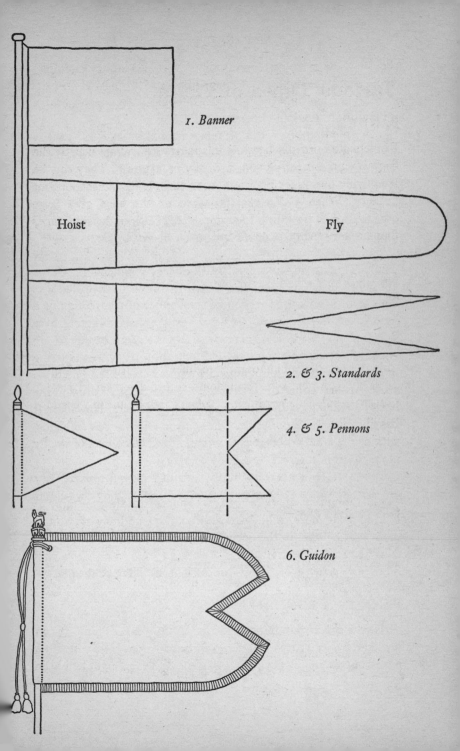

1. Banner

Hoist

Fly

2. & 3. Standards

4. & 5. Pennons

6. Guidon

particularly brave in battle the points were sometimes cut off thereby giving the pennon the shape of a small banner. He thus became a knight-banneret, which in medieval days made him more important than an ordinary knight.

In more modern times, the pennon was used by soldiers in the Lancer regiments. English Lancers carried red and white ones; the German Lancers, like the Uhlans, carried black and white ones.

GUIDON

A guidon is a type of pennon, but much broader. Its fly is slit and rounded.

Guidons are carried by some British cavalry regiments instead of the more usual shape of flag which in the army is called a 'colour'.

COLOUR

A 'colour' is the flag of an infantry regiment. It is banner-shaped and has the regiment's battle honours embroidered on it. Like the cavalry guidons, a regiment's 'colours' are beautifully made of silk and fringed with gold.

The staff from which it flies is usually called a 'colour pike'.

GONFANNON or GONFALON

The gonfannon is a square flag, like a banner, with three or more tails to it. It is more frequently seen on the Continent than in Britain. It either flies in the normal way or hangs from a crossbar fixed to the top of the staff.

The flags carried in religious processions are often of the gonfannon type.

ENSIGNS AND JACKS

At sea the flag flown from the staff at the stern of a ship is its ensign, while that flown in the bows is a jack. Nowadays the jack

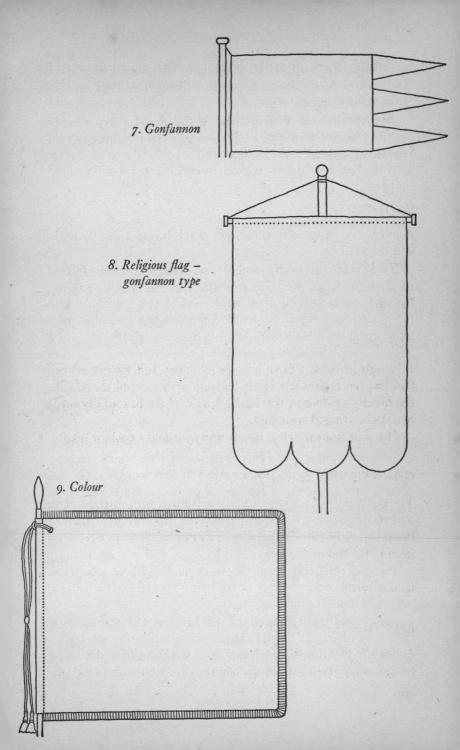

7. Gonfannon

8. Religious flag –
gonfannon type

9. Colour

is usually only flown when a ship is lying in harbour. Ensigns and jacks are used by most countries to distinguish their warships from their merchant ships.

For example, in Britain ships of the Royal Navy wear the White Ensign (see p. 35), while those of the merchant navy wear the Red Ensign.

Great Britain

ENGLAND

Until James I came to the throne in 1603 and united the kingdoms of England and Scotland, England's flag was plain white with a red cross on it. Traditionally this was the emblem of St George, who officially became England's patron saint early in the fifteenth century. The red cross on white had been used long before that because Richard I chose it as the emblem for the army which he took on his crusades to the Holy Land. England had long had a devotion to St George, a warrior saint, and King Richard placed his armies under St George's special protection.

This old flag of England, generally known as St George's flag, is not seen very often nowadays in this country. It is most usually seen flying over Protestant churches, and at international football matches when England is playing another country.

SCOTLAND

Scotland's flag is the white St Andrew's cross (called a 'saltire') on a blue background.

'The silver cross to Scotland dear' is very old. Legend dates it back to the reign of Angus II in the fourth century when some relics of St Andrew, who thenceforth became that country's patron saint, were brought to Scotland.

The flags of the United Kingdom

Top to bottom:
St George's Cross – England
St Andrew's Cross – Scotland
The Red Dragon – Wales
The Red Hand – Ulster

The other flag so often seen in Scotland is among the most beautiful and stately ever created. Poetically described as 'the ruddy lion ramping in his tressured field of gold' it is, strictly speaking, the royal banner of the Scottish monarch.

Thus when the blue and silver flag is flown it means 'here be Scotsmen', but when the red lion on the gold field is flown it means, or should mean, that either the Scottish sovereign or one of the principal Scottish officers of state is actually present in person where the flag is seen. The Lord Lyon King of Arms and the Secretary of State for Scotland, when acting in their official capacities, are among the few people entitled to the honour of flying the royal banner of Scotland.

WALES

The flag of Wales is a red dragon on a background divided horizontally white over green. The red dragon was the emblem of Cadwallader, who was one of the greatest Welsh princes. The colours of white and green are those of the Tudor family, which ruled England and Wales from 1485 to 1603.

NORTHERN IRELAND (Ulster)

The official flag of Northern Ireland is the Union Jack, but it has another semi-official one which it is allowed to fly. This is similar to the St George's cross of England – a red cross on a white background – but in the middle it has a white star with a red hand on it. The star has six points symbolizing the six counties of Northern Ireland. The red hand is an old emblem of Ulster and is associated with the O'Neills, who were one of the province's most prominent families.

THE UNION JACK

When Queen Elizabeth I died in 1603 she was succeeded on the throne of England by King James VI of Scotland, who thus

The evolution of the Union Jack or the 'Great Union'

became James I of England. Consequently the two nations were from that time on ruled over by the same sovereign. To symbolize this it was decided to join the flags of the two countries together in an emblematic way which would be acceptable to both peoples. Various ideas were submitted by the heralds of the day. The design which was eventually chosen is shown on p. 31. This arrangement remained until Ireland joined the Union of England and Scotland in 1801, when of course its flag had to be incorporated too.

As the flag used by Ireland was a red St Andrew's cross on a white background it was initially rather difficult to find a design which would not give offence by appearing to make Ireland seem inferior to both England and Scotland. So it was decided to rearrange the flag in the manner shown on p. 31, which is the way it has remained ever since.

Although this flag is universally called the 'Union Jack', strictly speaking its proper name is the 'Great Union'. It is really only a jack when flying from the jackstaff of a ship, which is the staff placed in the bows. It has been said that the name Jack when used in this context referred to the Scottish king, James VI, under whom the flag was first created – he always signed his name in the French form 'Jacques'.

THE COMPLAINT OF THE UNION JACK

'Those readers who know me – but, how few do – and have occasion to fly me, see that the broad white border of the diagonal cross is uppermost next to the staff. One word more – Hoist me *right up*; don't leave me flying four or five inches from the staff head. I have to fly half-mast sometimes, and it is hard to be made to do so on occasions of rejoicing.'
William Bland, *National Banners*, 1892.

GAZETTEER OF FLAGS

Afghanistan

Albania

Algeria

Andorra

Angola

Anguilla

Antigua

Argentina

Australia

Austria

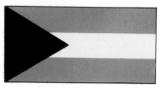

Bahamas

Bahrein

Bangladesh

Barbados

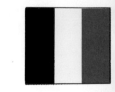

Belgium

Benin

Coat of Arms of Bermuda
flown on the fly of
the Red Ensign

Bolivia

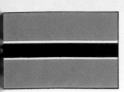

Botswana

Brazil

Shield of the
British Virgin Islands
flown on the fly of
the Blue Ensign

Brunei

Bulgaria

Burma

Burundi

Cameroon

Canada

Cape Verde Islands

Badge of the Cayman Islands
flown on the fly of
the Blue Ensign

Central African Empire

Chad

Badge of Alderney
flown at the centre of
St George's cross

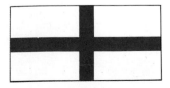

Guernsey

Jersey

Sark

Chile

China (Nationalist flag)

China (Communist flag)

Colombia

Comoro Republic

Congo

Costa Rica

Cuba

Cyprus

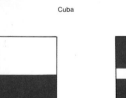

Czechoslovakia

Denmark

Coat of Arms of Dominica
flown on the fly of
the Blue Ensign

Dominican Republic

Ecuador

Ecuador's coat of arms
(sometimes shown on flag centre

Egypt

El Salvador

Equatorial Guinea

Ethiopia

Badge of the Falkland Islands
flown on the fly of
the Blue Ensign

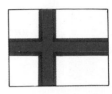

Faroe Islands

Fiji

Finland

France

Gabon

Gambia

East Germany

West Germany

Ghana

Badge of Gibraltar
flown on the fly of
the Blue Ensign

Shield of the Gilbert Islands
flown on the fly of
the Blue Ensign

Great Britain

Greece (national flag)

Greece (flag used outside the country)

Grenada

Guatemala

Guinea

Guinea Bissau

Guyana

Haiti

Holland

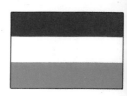

Honduras

Coat of Arms of Hong Kong
flown on the fly of
the Blue Ensign

Hungary

Iceland

India

Indonesia

Iran

Iraq

Ireland (Republic of Eire)

Isle of Man

Israel

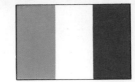

Italy

Jamaica

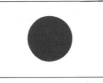

Japan

Jordan

Kampuchea

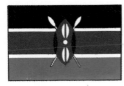

Kenya

North Korea

South Korea

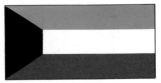

Kuwait

Laos

Lebanon

Lesotho

Liberia

Libya

Liechtenstein

Luxembourg

Malagasy Republic

Malawi

Malaysia

Maldive Islands

Mali

Malta GC

Mauritania

Mauritius

Mexico

Monaco

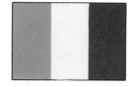

Mongolia

Shield of Montserrat
flown on the fly of
the Blue Ensign

Morocco

Mozambique

Nepal

Netherlands Antilles

New Zealand

Nicaragua

Niger

Nigeria

Norway

Oman

Pakistan

Panama

Papua and New Guinea

Paraguay

Peru

Philippine Islands

Poland

Portugal

Puerto Rico

Quatar

Rhodesia

Romania

Rwanda

Shield of St Helena
flown on the fly of
the Blue Ensign

St Kitts-Nevis

St Lucia

Shield of St Vincent
flown on the centre
of a blue flag

San Marino

Sao Tome e Principe

Saudi Arabia

Senegal

Seychelles

Sierra Leone

Sikkim

Singapore

Coat of Arms
of the Solomon Islands
flown on the fly of
the Blue Ensign

Somalia

South Africa

Spain

Sri Lanka

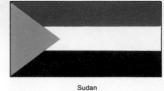

Sudan

Surinam

Swaziland

Sweden

Switzerland

Syria

Tanzania

Thailand

Tibet

Togo

Tonga

Trinidad and Tobago

Tunisia

Turkey

Shield of Turks & Caicos Islands
flown on the fly of
the Blue Ensign

Uganda

United Arab Republic

United States of America

Upper Volta

Uruguay

USSR

Vatican City

Venezuela

Vietnam

Western Samoa

Yemen Arab Republic

Yemen (Peoples' Democratic Republic of)

Yugoslavia

Zaire

Zambia

The big red, gold and blue flag with lions and a harp on it, which flies over Buckingham Palace or wherever the Queen happens to be, is usually known as the Royal Standard, though, as I've already mentioned, strictly speaking it is a banner.

At the moment it is divided into four quarters. The top left and bottom right-hand quarters show the royal arms of England. These are red with three gold lions. The top right-hand quarter is gold with the red lion of Scotland. The bottom left-hand corner shows the royal arms of Ireland, a blue background with a silver-stringed gold harp, which has been retained to symbolize Ulster.

The royal arms of these three countries put together show, symbolically, that the Queen is not only Queen of England but Queen of Scotland and Northern Ireland as well. It indicates that the Union of the Crowns of these countries is centred in one person, in exactly the same way as the Union Jack symbolizes that the union of these countries is centred in one parliament.

Before Ireland joined the United Kingdom in 1801 the Union Jack had a slightly different appearance to that which it has now. The royal banner has undergone similar changes during its history.

From the days of Richard I until Edward II the royal banner of England was a simple red flag with the three gold lions (1).

In 1340 Edward III claimed to be King of France, so he added the arms of their kings, blue scattered with a lot of gold fleurs-de-lis, to his standard (2). To show that he considered France the most important of his countries he placed the French part in the place of honour – the top left-hand corner. The French 'quartering' was later slightly changed so that only three lilies appeared on it.

On the accession of James I in 1603 the royal arms of Scotland and Ireland were added, so that the banner looked like this (3).

When England and Scotland, which had been separate countries, although ruled by the same sovereign, were joined

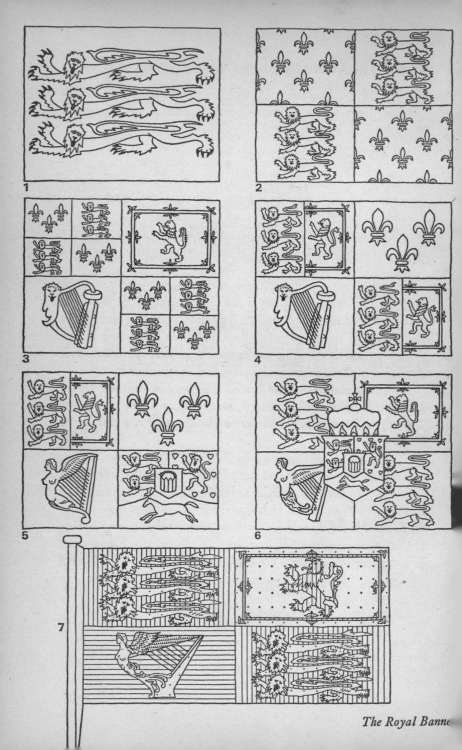

The Royal Banne

together as the United Kingdom under one parliament in 1707, Queen Anne changed the royal banner to show England and Scotland jointly in the place of honour and the lilies of France were moved to second place (4).

When the Hanoverians came to the throne in 1714, the royal banner was altered to include their arms (5).

As a friendly gesture to Napoleon, George III, in 1802, formally renounced all claim to the French throne. To symbolize this the lilies of France were removed from the royal banner. At the same time the arms of Hanover were put into a shield shape in the middle of the flag (6). After the Congress of Vienna in 1816, when Hanover became a kingdom instead of an electorate, a crown replaced the cap.

Women were not allowed to rule over Hanover, so when Queen Victoria succeeded to the throne of England in 1837, the throne of Hanover passed to her uncle, Ernest, Duke of Cumberland, and the arms of Hanover were taken off the British Royal Banner, leaving it in the state in which it remains today (7).

THE WHITE ENSIGN

This is the St George's flag of England with the Union Jack in the canton. It is the official flag of the Royal Navy and may only be used by ships belonging to it, i.e., those ships which have HMS before their name – HMS *Eagle*, for example.

THE BLUE ENSIGN

The Blue Ensign is a blue flag with the Union Jack in the canton. It is flown or, as they say at sea, worn, by ships which, although not belonging to the Royal Navy, have some sort of official status. It nearly always has a distinctive badge in the fly denoting what the official organization is, whether it is the Sea Cadet Corps, the Consular Service or one of the many other public service bodies. Some yacht clubs are also allowed to use it.

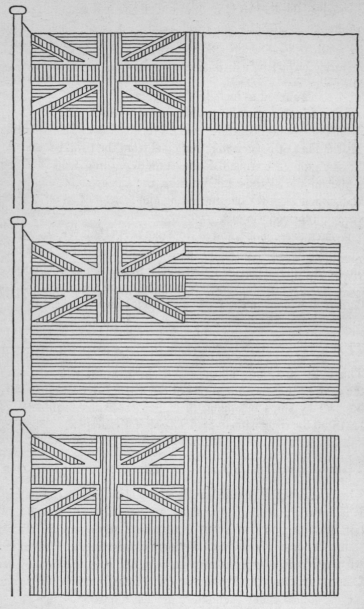

The Ensigns

THE RED ENSIGN

This is a red flag with the Union Jack in the canton. It is flown by all British merchant ships and by any ship or boat which is privately owned by a British subject. It is nicknamed the 'Red Duster'.

The United States of America

THE STARS AND STRIPES

When the United States declared themselves independent of Britain on 4 July 1776 they adopted a new flag to replace the Union Jack. They chose the Stars and Stripes. To start with the number of stars and stripes varied, but in 1818 it was decided that there should be thirteen stripes (seven red and six white) to commemorate the original thirteen States which formed the

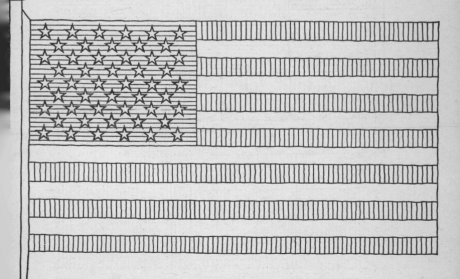

Union and on the blue canton there were to be as many stars as there were States in the Union. There are now fifty States in the Union so the canton has fifty stars on it. The stars were originally chosen to signify that a bright new constellation had arisen among the nations.

The United States has strict rules governing the use of their flag. For instance it may not be used for advertising, and American citizens have to pledge their 'allegiance to the flag of the United States of America and to the Republic for which it stands . . .'

THE CONFEDERATE FLAG

During the American Civil War the Southern States had two main flags. The civil flag was a horizontal tricolour, red over white over red with a circle of seven white stars on a blue canton. The battle flag was red with a white-edged blue St Andrew's

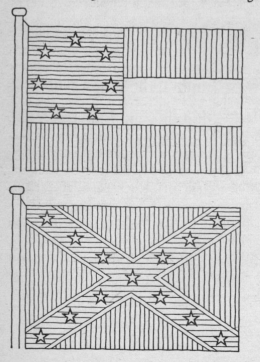

cross. On each arm of the cross were four stars with an additional one in its centre making seventeen stars in all. Sometimes this flag had a narrow white border.

The Confederate army suffered a crushing defeat at Gettysburg in July 1864 and finally surrendered at Appomattox in 1865. Since then this flag, although occasionally seen on commemorative occasions in the States which once formed the Confederacy, has had no official significance in America.

The Cross, the Crescent and the Star

The cross is the symbol of Christianity, and is found in the flags of so many of the older European countries because in one form or another it was usually the emblem of the country's patron saint.

Although the crescent is the symbol of Mohammedanism, it is said that its origins go back to the year 339 BC when the Greeks were besieging Byzantium. One night they attempted a surprise attack on the city, but the crescent moon rose and its light gave away their position, enabling the defenders to save the city. Thereafter the people of Byzantium used the crescent as their emblem. Byzantium later became Constantinople (and is now Istanbul) and when the Mohammedans captured the city in 1453 they took the symbol for their own and have kept it ever since.

The red star has been adopted as the emblem of many Communist countries. Blood red is the colour of defiance and revolution, but the use of the star in this context may have Napoleonic origins. At one time Napoleon's politics were anti-Christian and seeking an emblem to replace the cross of Christianity he chose the star.

Eastern Flags

The Muslim peoples used flags quite early on. Captain Barra-clough RN in his valuable work *Flags of the World* mentions that evidence exists of standards being used by the grandsons of Mohammed (*c*. 570–632). These were triangular flags with fringes attached to a staff. One was plain green while the other had a Mohammedan double-bladed dagger on it.

Green is the Mohammedan sacred colour, which is why it is so frequently found in flags of the predominantly Muslim countries of the Middle East.

These usually include red, black and white as well. These colours are believed to commemorate some of the great Moham-medan dynastic families: red for the Hashemites; black the Abbasids, and white the Omayhads. Green is also the colour of another famous Muslim family, the Fatimid.

Miscellaneous Flags and Oddities

Sometimes flags of one colour only are seen. Here are some examples of them and what they mean, or have meant in the past.

YELLOW

A yellow flag is flown when serious disease is present. If a ship is seen flying a yellow flag it is known as being 'in quarantine'. It indicates that one or more people on board are suffering from cholera, yellow fever or some other serious infectious disease.

WHITE

This is the flag of truce or surrender.

RED

A red flag, or 'bloody colours' as it was often called, means danger. It is also the symbol of mutiny aboard ship or of revolution ashore. It has been the emblematic colour of socialism and Communism since the days of the French Revolution in 1789. It was also the flag of the D'Albret family and flew at Agincourt because a D'Albret was Constable of France at the time. Most of the socialists and Communists who fly a red flag today would be surprised to know that it also commemorates a family famous in the French annals of chivalry!

BLACK

A black flag usually has a rather sinister meaning: for instance it flew from pirate ships, often with the white skull and crossbones motif added. It was the signal for 'No quarter', meaning that anyone captured during or after a battle would be killed. Until quite recently a black flag was flown over a prison when an execution had taken place. The Mohammedan peoples used it to symbolize a declaration of war.

GREEN

Green is the signal of safety, but at sea green flags are used to mark the sites of dangerous wrecks.

BLUE PETER

This is a blue flag with a white square in the middle. Ships fly it to indicate they are about to sail.

BLACK AND WHITE

A black and white chequered flag is waved when the winner of a motor race crosses the finishing line.

Famous Flags

THE CHAPE DE ST MARTIN

Despite the confusion which prevailed in Europe during the Dark Ages, there was one notable flag of the period, the Chape de St Martin. This was supposed to have been the hood which had belonged to St Martin of Tours, who had been a soldier before taking Orders and later becoming a bishop. It was of plain blue cloth and belonged to the Abbey of Marmoutiers.

Having a premonition that he would be victorious if he had it with him, Clovis borrowed the hood from the monks and used it as his standard during his great and successful battle against the Goths in 507. Thereafter many French kings, including Charle-

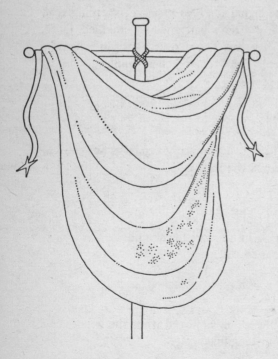

magne, fought under it and it is said to have often led France to
victory. To all intents and purposes it was the flag of the Caro-
lingian dynasty of France, which lasted until the death of Louis V
in 987.

THE ORIFLAMME

With the rise of the Capet family which ruled France from 987
until the French Revolution in 1789 the Chape de St Martin fell
into disuse, the new dynasty adopting the Oriflamme in its place.

Originally of plain scarlet cloth or silk, it was later embroidered
with golden tongues of flame. It usually had three tails ending in
green tassels.

As it had originally been the banner of the Abbey of St Denis,
near Paris, it was normally kept there in peacetime, only coming
out in time of war.

It was first used by Louis VI in 1124. The last time it was seen

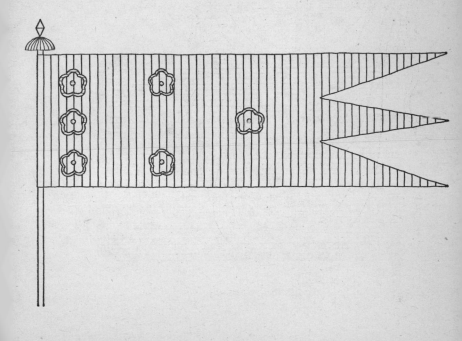

is supposed to have been at Agincourt in 1415, but the English chroniclers may have mistaken it for the plain red banner of Charles D'Albret, the Constable of France (see p. 41).

Carrying the Oriflamme, which was always borne immediately before the king, was one of the highest honours in medieval France.

THE FLEURS-DE-LIS

Up to the French Revolution the flag of France was a very beautiful one. It was blue with three gold fleurs-de-lis on it. The origin of the fleurs-de-lis is not quite certain but it seems they were used as early as AD 496.

In early times there were a lot of fleurs-de-lis on the flag, but in 1365 Charles V ordered that, in honour of the Blessed Trinity, only three should be shown.

The personal flag of the French kings of later days had the three fleurs-de-lis on a white background.

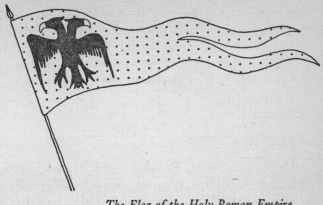

The Flag of the Holy Roman Empire

THE HOLY ROMAN EMPIRE

This was the name used for the empire of Charlemagne, 742–814. In 962 it was applied to the German Empire, and existed until 1806 when Napoleon suppressed it.

Its flag was a famous one, and is often seen in books with pictures relating to that period. It was yellow with a black eagle on it, a double-headed eagle.

OLYMPIC GAMES FLAG

Every four years when the Olympic Games are held the flag of the Olympic Games is flown in the stadium and arenas where the various games are taking place. It is one of the best known of modern international flags.

The background of the flag is white; on it are five interlinked circles, of blue, gold, black, green and red respectively, forming a chain. It has been suggested that this arrangement symbolizes the linking of the peoples of the five continents into the single family of sportsmen.

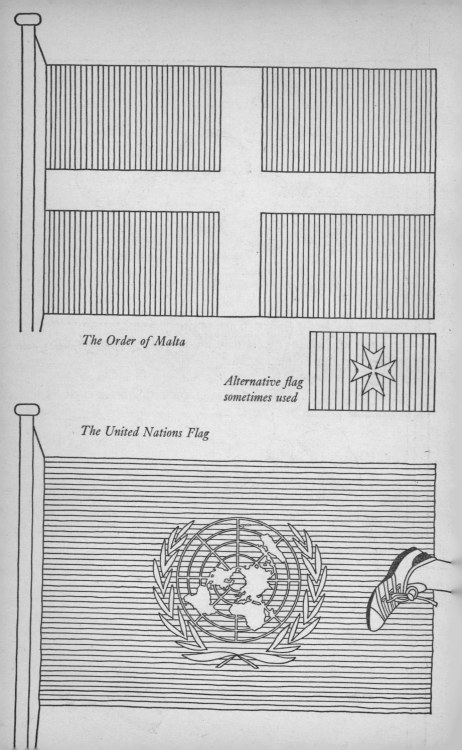

The Order of Malta

Alternative flag
sometimes used

The United Nations Flag

The Flag of the Olympic Games

ORDER OF MALTA

The full title is the Sovereign Military Order of the Knights Hospitaller of St John of Jerusalem, of Rhodes and of Malta. Being a Sovereign Order it has its own ruler, the Prince Grand Master, and exchanges ambassadors with many countries. In Italy and other places, where the Order's sovereign nature is recognized, the Prince Grand Master is treated with all the courtesies due to a sovereign head of state. Its flag, which may date back to 1113, is possibly the oldest in use. It is red with a white St George's cross on it, and can be seen flying over the Order's headquarters which are now in Rome. To differentiate it from the Dannebrog (see 'Denmark'), a red flag with a white eight-pointed St John's cross (sometimes called a Maltese cross) may sometimes be used.

THE UNITED NATIONS ORGANISATION FLAG

After the Second World War the United Nations Organisation was formed by representatives from practically every country in the world, its intention being to keep the world at peace. The Organisation has its own flag which is blue with a map of the world between two olive branches on it, all in white. The olive branch is a symbol of peace.

THE RED CROSS

After the battle of Solferino in 1859, in which there were terrible casualties, a Swiss, called Jean Dunant, persuaded most governments to agree that those who had been wounded in war, and the medical services, should be regarded as neutrals. At the Geneva Convention of 1864 it was also agreed that the medical services should have their own distinguishing flag, and as Jean Dunant was Swiss it was decided that the flag should be like Switzerland's (see p. 98), with the colours reversed, i.e. a red cross on a white background.

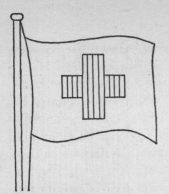

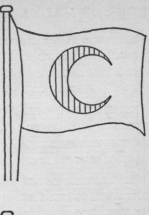

As the Muslim countries consider the Cross to be a purely Christian symbol their medical services have a white flag with a red crescent on it. Those of Iran, though, have a white flag with a red lion carrying a sword in front of a red rising sun.

Tricolours

The use of a tricolour flag by a country often means that that country has gained its independence from another, either by peaceful or war-like means.

Tricolours, being of a very simple design, are easy to make and can be produced very quickly. They can equally rapidly be unstitched and separated into innocent pieces of coloured cloth, which would not be possible with some of the more complex flags, such as the Stars and Stripes or the Royal Standard!

It has been said that the new countries in Africa which now fly vertical tricolours were once under French rule, while those flying horizontal ones were formerly parts of the British Empire. Broadly speaking, this may be so, but it is by no means an invariable rule, so it should not be relied on as a sure guide.

Flags in Churches

When you are in churches like St Paul's Cathedral and Westminster Abbey, you may see a number of splendid heraldic flags hanging next to each other in a side chapel. These are the banners

of important knights of the great Orders of Chivalry – the Order of the Garter, the Order of the Bath, and so on.

Actually, these are the family flags of the individual knights and can also sometimes be seen flying over their private homes in much the same way as the Queen flies the royal family's flag over Buckingham Palace.

When the Order concerned has a big ceremony you may see these banners being carried in procession behind the knights by their individual standard bearers.

Other flags to be seen in churches include old 'colours' (see p. 27), which have been 'laid up' by their regiments. Colours are 'laid up' when they have become too fragile for further use, or when a regiment is disbanded.

51

In Britain the banners of the knights of some of the Orders of Chivalry may be seen in the following churches:

The Order of the Garter   *St George's Chapel, Windsor*
The Order of the Thistle   *St Giles's Cathedral, Edinburgh*
The Order of the Bath   *Westminster Abbey*
The Order of St Michael and St George   *St Paul's Cathedral*
The Royal Victorian Order   *The Chapel Royal of the Savoy*
The Order of the British Empire   *St Paul's Cathedral*

Although there are no longer any Knights of St Patrick, the banners of some former ones still hang in St Patrick's Cathedral, Dublin.

The Standard Bearers

Throughout military history it has always been considered a great honour to be entrusted with the privilege of carrying a flag or standard.

In the armies of Imperial Rome the man who carried it was known as the *signifer*. He was usually of the rank of centurion and used to wear a special cap made out of a leopard's head.

In the Middle Ages such a man was called the standard bearer. At Agincourt the royal standard bearer was Sir John Codrington. The King marked his valour by awarding him a distinctive mark to be borne on his

A standard bearer

coat of arms, which his branch of the Codrington family still bears today.

In modern times the officer in the Brigade of Guards who carries the regiment's colour is called the Ensign to the Colour. He is usually a second-lieutenant and is always to be seen at the Changing of the Guard or on the Queen's birthday parade at the ceremony called Trooping the Colour.

During this ceremony the Ensign carries the colour slowly along the ranks of soldiers enabling them to see it closely so that they can recognize it on future occasions.

Naval Signalling Flags

Various systems have been used through the ages, but the system presently in use by the Royal Navy was prepared in accordance with NATO requirements. In essence it comprises one flag for each of the twenty-six letters of the alphabet, ten numeral flags (nought to nine), and about thirty-eight other ones used for special purposes, making about seventy-four for use in signalling.

The most famous naval signal in history was given by Lord Nelson on 21 October 1805 just as the battle of Trafalgar was about to start.

Flag Rank

Flag rank is a naval term. It refers to admirals in general, because only these officers are allowed to fly, or 'wear', a flag on their ships denoting their rank. From this comes the term flag ship – or admiral's ship. A flag lieutenant is an admiral's aide.

The flags (see p. 56) of the different ranks of admiral are:
(1) Admiral of the Fleet
(2) Admiral
(3) Vice Admiral
(4) Rear Admiral

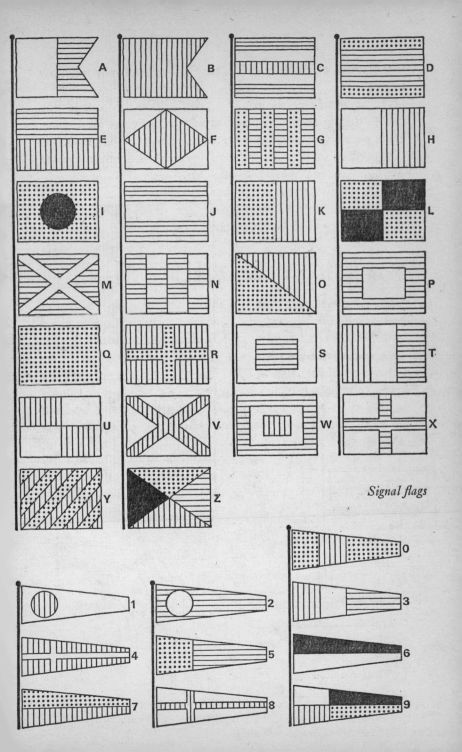

Signal flags

Admirals' flags

1

2

3

4

Omens of Disaster

The coronation of James II, the last of the Stuart kings (1684–8), was attended by so many ill omens that even a television commentator of modern times might have been shaken. The crown itself fitted him so badly that when the Archbishop of Canterbury placed it on James's head it seemed to totter and would have fallen to the ground had Henry Sydney not come to the rescue and steadied it. Later in the day, right in front of James, Sir Charles Dymoke, the King's Champion, was thrown from his horse and lay prostrate on the ground pinned beneath it, unable to rise. These events however were only witnessed by the nobility and the privileged few who actually attended the coronation ceremonies. The evil omen which was seen by many of the people of London was the one which concerned a flag. Flying over the Tower of London that day was the huge Royal Standard, the king's own personal flag. Just as the message arrived at the Tower to fire the guns to let the people know their king was well and truly crowned, a tempestuous gust of wind tore the flag in half and the fly, which included in it the part symbolizing the Stuart's connection with the country, was tossed to the ground.

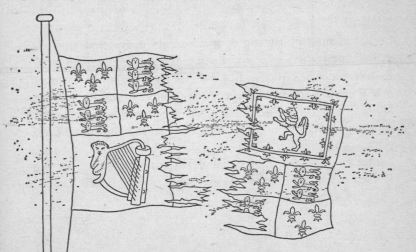

Three years later, in 1688, James II was forced to flee the country. When his daughter, Queen Anne, died in 1714 the Stuarts ceased to rule Great Britain.

A similar event occurred on 24 June 1875 in America. As General George Custer, Commander of the 7th Cavalry Brigade of the US Army, was sitting outside his tent in the still air of that hot summer's evening, making the final plans for his attack on the Sioux Indians, at the Little Big Horn the following day, he heard a splintering noise behind him. On looking round he was horrified to see that the nearby flag pole had quite inexplicably snapped in two, and the brigade's colours were lying in the dust.

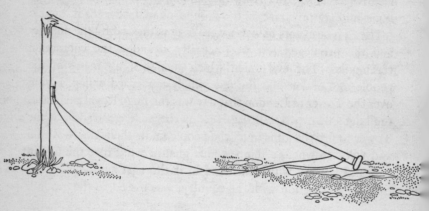

Some of his aides, who had been distinctly uneasy about the likely outcome of the fight, immediately considered this as a supernatural warning of impending disaster and begged Custer to reconsider his plans. But the General remained adamant. When battle was joined the next day Custer found he had been led into a trap. Instead of the small body of Indians he had expected to engage his party of about 250 men, they found themselves surrounded by between 3,000 and 5,000 of the enemy. Custer and his troops were slaughtered to a man. Not one survived. Like its colours the previous evening, the whole of Custer's army lay in the dust of North Dakota.

THE FAIRY FLAG

The McLeods of Dunvegan in the Isle of Skye have a flag called the Bratach Sith, which means the Fairy Flag. It is said to have been given to them by the wife of the fourth chief of the clan. He lived in the fourteenth century and his wife was reputed to have been a fairy. The legend has it that she gave it to her husband as a parting present before returning to her home in fairyland.

She told him that if the McLeods were in mortal danger from their enemies and waved the flag they would be saved, but that it could only be used three times. So far it has been successfully used twice, in battles against the McDonalds, once in 1490 and again in 1520.

The Bratach Sith can still be seen at Dunvegan Castle. It is of delicate brown silk, which may have come from Damascus or Rhodes, so in reality it was probably brought back by a McLeod who had been on a pilgrimage or crusade to the Middle East.

GAZETTEER

AFGHANISTAN

This country, on the north-west frontier of Pakistan, has a black, red and green flag. The bottom half of the flag is green while the top half comprises two horizontal stripes of equal width showing black over red. In the canton is the Afghanistan state emblem, an eagle between two sheaves of wheat and the rays of the sun all in yellow.

ALBANIA

Albania is a little Communist country, south of Yugoslavia. Its flag is red with a black double-headed eagle on it. Just above the eagle is a gold-edged red star. The double-headed eagle was the symbol of a great Albanian hero called Skanderbeg. In the Albanian language the word for Albania (Shquipera) means 'Land of the Eagles', so the eagle emblem is an appropriate one.

ALGERIA

This country used to belong to France but became independent in 1962. Its flag is divided vertically, green and white, with a red crescent and star in the centre.

ANDORRA

This is a tiny country, nestling in the Pyrenees between France and Spain. Its flag combines the colours of its two big neighbours: the blue of France, the gold of Spain, and red which is common to both. For so small a country it has quite a number of ways of displaying its flag. Sometimes the blue, gold and red are shown horizontally and at other times vertically. In the middle section you might see either the Andorran coat of arms or a little crown.

ANGOLA

Angola used to be governed by Portugal but recently became an independent state when it took a new flag. This was introduced on 11 November 1975 and is a horizontal bicolour of red over black with a five-pointed yellow star, a yellow *machete* (a type of knife) and half a yellow cog-wheel in the centre.

ANGUILLA

This is an island in the Caribbean Sea administered by Britain. In 1967 it began unofficially to use a white flag with a narrow light blue stripe at the foot. On the white part are three interlocking orange dolphins. The white symbolizes peace, the blue the sea and the dolphins strength and endurance.

ANTIGUA

One of the Leeward Islands in the West Indies. It has a very distinctive flag: red with an upside-down triangle of black, blue and white. On the black part a gold sun rises. The base of the triangle lies along the top edge of the flag.

ARGENTINA

This big South American country has a horizontal tricolour of light blue over white over light blue. On the white part is a gold sun with a face on it. The light blue and white is said to commemorate the colours worn by those nationals who won independence for the country.

AUSTRALIA

Australia has a blue flag with a Union Jack in the canton and five small white stars in the fly. These represent the Southern Cross, a constellation in the sky which can only be seen south of the equator. Under the Union Jack is one big star called the Commonwealth Star.

Australia also has another flag called the Commonwealth Flag which incorporates the flags of the six states of Australia: New South Wales, Victoria, Queensland, Western Australia, South Australia and Tasmania.

AUSTRIA

In its long history Austria has used many flags. Among the oldest and most famous is the one it uses now. This is a red over white over red tricolour. This flag has an interesting history. In 1191 Leopold of Austria, the Duke of Bebenburg, was in a battle and got terribly wounded. When he took his surcoat off it was entirely red with his blood except round his middle where his belt had been. This part was still white. Consequently he decreed that henceforward Austria should have a red flag with a white band across the middle.

Another famous Austrian flag in days gone by was that of the Holy Roman Empire. This was gold with a black double-headed eagle on it (see p. 45).

BAHAMAS

The Bahamas are a group of islands in the Atlantic, a little east of Cuba. They became independent of Britain in 1973 and took a new flag, a horizontal tricolour showing blue over yellow over blue with a black triangle in the hoist. The blue represents the sea, the yellow the sands of the Bahaman islands and the black the unity of the country's people.

BAHREIN

This is a small group of islands in the Persian Gulf. Its flag is red with a white band in the hoist which has a saw-tooth edge.

BANGLADESH

When India and Pakistan were re-formed as two separate countries in 1948 Bengal became East Pakistan, but in 1971 it won its independence, took a new name, Bangladesh, and adopted a new flag; this is green with a red roundel on it.

BARBADOS

An island in the West Indies. When it became independent within the British Commonwealth in 1966 it adopted a new flag, which is a vertical tricolour of blue, yellow and blue stripes. On the central yellow stripe is the head of a trident in black.

BELGIUM

The flag is a tricolour of black, yellow and red vertical stripes. They are taken from the colours of the coat of arms of Brabant.

BENIN

This used to be a part of French West Africa called Dahomey, which gained its independence in 1960. In December 1975 it changed its name to Benin, adopting a new flag at the same time. This is green with a red five-pointed star in the canton.

BERMUDA

A beautiful little group of islands belonging to Britain, set like a jewel in the western Atlantic. Its people are very loyal to the English Crown. Its flag is the Red Ensign with the islands' coat of arms in the fly. This is a white shield with a grassy mound at the bottom; seated on this is a red lion holding another shield, which shows a storm-tossed ship near some rocks.

BOLIVIA

A country in South America. Its flag is a horizontal tricolour of red over yellow over green with the national coat of arms on the yellow part. It is thought that the red denotes the animal life of the country, the yellow and green its mineral and vegetable resources.

BOTSWANA

This used to be a British Protectorate in Africa, called Bechuanaland. When it became independent in 1966 it adopted a light blue flag with a horizontal black stripe edged with white.

BRAZIL

This large South American country has a green flag with a yellow diamond in the middle. On the diamond is a blue globe studded with stars and a motto *Ordem e Progresio* ('Order and Progress'). It is thought that the green and yellow colours represent Brazil's jungles and minerals.

BRITISH VIRGIN ISLANDS

These are in the West Indies. Their flag is the Blue Ensign with a shield in the fly. This is green with a woman and twelve lamps all in white. Underneath the shield is a scroll with the word *Vigilate* on it. This means 'Be watchful'.

BRUNEI

A country on the island of Borneo. Its flag is yellow with a diagonal stripe from top left to bottom right which is itself divided diagonally, white over black. In red in the centre is the country's emblem which consists of a kind of double-tiered tower with wings at the top. Surrounding the tower is a crescent, on either side of which is a hand pointing upwards. On a scroll underneath the crescent is the motto 'Always serve with the guidance of God'.

BULGARIA

One of the Communist countries in south-east Europe. Its flag is a horizontal tricolour of white over green over red. These are probably derived from the colours of its near neighbour, Hungary. In the canton (top left-hand corner) of the Bulgarian flag is the country's symbol. This is a lion enclosed between two sheaves of corn on top of which is a red star.

BURMA

One of the countries of south-east Asia. It used to have a peacock as its emblem. It became independent from Britain in 1948, and in 1973 adopted a red flag with a blue canton on which are a cog-wheel and ears of rice within a circle of fourteen five-pointed stars, all coloured white.

BURUNDI

Burundi is in east Africa and used to belong to Belgium. When it gained its independence in 1962 it adopted quite a different flag. It has a white St Andrew's cross at the centre of which is a white circle on which are three deep-red stars. The background is also deep red at the top and bottom while the sides are green.

CAMEROON

The Cameroon Republic is in Africa. It was a German colony until the First World War, when it was taken over by Britain and France. It became independent in 1961 and has a vertical tri-colour of green, red and yellow. On the central red stripe is a yellow five-pointed star.

CANADA

For many years Canada used the Red Ensign (a red flag with the Union Jack in the canton) with Canada's coat of arms in the fly.

Although Canada is the oldest of the British Dominions, its people decided, in 1965, to abolish this symbolic tie with its mother country by having a new flag. It chose a very simple and distinctive design: a red maple leaf on a white background between two broad red vertical bands.

Canada has two others flags which are often seen inside the country. They are the Provincial flags of Quebec and Nova Scotia. The Quebec flag is blue with a white cross between four white fleurs-de-lis. Many Quebecois are of French descent so the fleurs-de-lis and the blue are emblematic of their tie with France, while white was the colour of the Bourbons, the french royal family. Thus the incorporation of white in the Quebec flag is a discreet but pleasing mark of respect to one of the most distinguished families in history.

The flag of Nova Scotia ('New Scotland') recalls the Province's connections with Scotland. It is basically the flag of Scotland reversed, namely a blue St Andrew's cross on a white background. In the centre is the royal coat of arms of Scotland – a red lion rampant surrounded by a red double tressure on a gold shield.

CAPE VERDE ISLANDS

These are a group of islands in the Atlantic Ocean off the west coast of Africa. They used to belong to Portugal, but recently became independent. Their flag has a yellow over green bicolour fly with a red hoist on which is a wreath of green leaves, embodying on each side a brown and yellow fruit and enclosing a five-pointed black star above a yellow shell.

CAYMAN ISLANDS

The Cayman Islands in the Caribbean belong to Britain and have as their flag the Blue Ensign with their badge in the fly. This comprises a white roundel on which is a coat of arms. The shield has three five-pointed green stars edged with gold on a background of three white and three blue wavy lines. The top is red with a gold lion. Above the shield is a green turtle in front of some palm leaves. On a scroll below the shield is the motto: 'He hath founded it upon the Seas'.

CENTRAL AFRICAN EMPIRE

This country has a very colourful flag. It comprises four horizontal stripes, blue over white over green over yellow with a vertical red stripe in the centre. In the left-hand corner of the blue stripe at the top of the flag is a yellow star.

CHAD

Once part of French Equatorial Africa, Chad became independent in 1960. Its flag is a blue, yellow and red vertical tricolour.

THE CHANNEL ISLANDS

Alderney. Flies the St George's cross with at the centre a gold-bordered green circle on which is a crowned gold lion holding a sprig of leaves.

68

Guernsey. Flies the St George's cross.
Jersey. Flies the St Patrick's cross.
Sark. Flies the St George's cross with two red lions in the canton, the lower half of the lower lion being in the arm of the cross.

CHILE

Chile is in South America. Its flag is based on that of the United States. It has two horizontal stripes, white over red, and a single white star on a blue canton.

CHINA

China has two flags, one used in Formosa by the Nationalist Government and one used by the Communists on the mainland.

The Nationalist flag is red with a white sun on a blue canton. The Chinese Communist flag is also red with one big and four small yellow stars in the canton.

Both these Chinese flags are quite new. The Nationalist one was first used in 1912. The Communist one became official in 1949.

Until 1912, and for centuries before that, when China still had an emperor, the imperial banner was usually swallow-tailed in shape. It was coloured yellow with blue edging and often had a black dragon in the centre.

COLOMBIA

One of the smaller South American countries. The top half of the flag is yellow and the lower half has two horizontal stripes, dark blue over red. This flag is very similar to that of another South American country, Ecuador.

It has been said that these colours symbolize 'Golden America separated by the blue sea from bloodthirsty Spain'.

COMORO REPUBLIC

This consists of four small islands off the coast of Mozambique. They became independent of France in July 1975. Its flag is red over green, the red part being about twice as wide as the green. In the canton is a white crescent and four white five-pointed stars.

CONGO

There used to be two countries in Africa called by this name. The country which was formerly the French Congo is now known as the People's Republic of Congo and has its capital at Brazzaville. Its flag is red with the country's emblem in the fly. This is a crossed mattock (a type of axe) and hammer above which is a five-pointed star, all in yellow, surrounded by a wreath of green fronds.

The former Belgian Congo is now called Zaire.

COSTA RICA

Once one of the countries forming the Central American Federation. Its flag is white with a narrow horizontal blue stripe at the top and bottom and a broad red one in the middle.

CUBA

An island in the Caribbean. Its flag is blue with two horizontal white stripes. In the hoist is a red triangle on which is a white star.

CYPRUS

Cyprus, an island in the Mediterranean, became independent from Britain in 1960. Its flag is now white with a map of the island in yellow above two olive branches in green. Olive branches are symbols of peace.

CZECHOSLOVAKIA

A central European country formed after the 1914–18 war from three provinces – Bohemia, Moravia and Slovakia – which had belonged to Austria. Its flag, two horizontal stripes white over red and a blue triangle in the hoist, recall two of these: the red and white of Bohemia and the blue of Moravia.

DENMARK

Denmark's flag has a white cross on a red background. The vertical part of the cross lies off centre towards the hoist. It is called the Dannebrog, which means the 'Strength of Denmark'. There is a tradition that its use originated from a vision seen in the sky by King Waldemar of Denmark in the year 1219 just before a battle. The flag of Denmark is supposed to be the oldest of all flags now in current use, but this may be due to confusion with the flag of the Order of Malta, which also has a white cross on a red background. The Order of Malta was founded in 1113, over a century before the first use of the Dannebrog.

DOMINICA

Dominica is in the Caribbean close to Haiti and belongs to Britain. Its flag is the Blue Ensign with the country's coat of arms in the fly. The shield is quartered yellow and blue; on it are a coconut palm, an edible toad, a canoe and a banana tree. On each side of the shield is a green parrot. Above the shield is the crest which is a gold lion of England on a rocky mound. Below the shield is the motto: '*Apres Bondie c'est la terre*', which in the local dialect means 'After the Good God we love the earth'.

DOMINICAN REPUBLIC

The eastern part of a Caribbean island of which Haiti forms the western part. Dominica's flag is quartered blue and red with a white cross at the centre, on which is the country's coat of arms.

ECUADOR

A South American country. Its flag is very similar to Colombia's. Its top half is yellow and the lower half is divided horizontally blue over red. In the centre of the flag is Ecuador's coat of arms on top of which is a large bird called a condor with its wings outspread. On the merchant flag the coat of arms is left off. The only way then of distinguishing it from the flag of Colombia is by looking at the shade of the blue stripe. Ecuador's blue is a light blue, while Colombia's is dark.

EGYPT

Egypt has had a number of different flags. Its present one is a horizontal tricolour of red over white over black; it has a yellow eagle emblem in the centre above a scroll on which, written in Arabic lettering, are the words 'Arab Republic of Egypt'.

EIRE see IRELAND, p. 80

EL SALVADOR

El Salvador formerly belonged, with Honduras and Guatemala, to the United Provinces of Central America. It has a horizontal blue over white over blue tricolour. On the white stripe is the country's coat of arms.

EQUATORIAL GUINEA

This is on the west coast of Africa. Formerly Spanish Guinea, it became independent in 1968. It has a horizontal tricolour flag of green over white over red with a blue triangle in the hoist. On the central white stripe is a blue shield with a cotton tree on it. Above the shield are six gold stars and below it the country's motto, which, in English, means 'Unity, Peace and Justice'.

ETHIOPIA

Ethiopia is in Africa and used to be called Abyssinia. It has a horizontal tricolour of green over yellow over red.

FALKLAND ISLANDS

The Falkland Islands are in the south Atlantic and are part of the Commonwealth. The flag is the Blue Ensign with the islands' badge in the fly. This shows a shield on a white roundel. The shield is blue with a white ram standing on a green mound in the upper part and a three-masted sailing ship in front of three wavy white lines in the lower part. Below the shield is a scroll bearing the motto: 'Desire the Right'.

FAROE ISLANDS

These islands between Scotland and Iceland come under Danish rule, but have their own flag. It is a red St George's cross edged with blue on a white background.

FIJI

A group of islands in the Pacific, east of Australia and north of New Zealand, part of the British Commonwealth. Its flag shows its links with Britain; since 1970 it has been light blue with a Union Jack in the canton and the island's coat of arms in the fly. The coat of arms is white with a red St George's cross on it. In the four quarters formed by the cross are sugar canes, a coconut tree, a dove carrying an olive branch in its beak and a bunch of bananas on a branch. The top of the shield is red with a gold lion holding a coconut tree in its front paws.

FINLAND

Finland gained its independence from Russia in 1917 and adopted a white flag with a blue cross on it, which, like those of Denmark and the other Scandinavian countries, has the vertical arm off centre towards the hoist. The colours, blue and white, are emblematic of the lakes and snowfields of Finland.

FRANCE

With the Union Jack of Britain and the Stars and Stripes of America, the French flag is one of the best known in the world. It is the most famous of all tricolours. Its three vertical stripes are blue in the hoist, white in the centre and red in the fly.

The red and blue commemorate the colours on the coat of arms of Paris and the white commemorates the Bourbon family, which ruled France from 1589 to 1848 with a gap during the French Revolution.

Before the French Revolution broke out in 1789, the French flag was blue and had heraldic lilies called fleurs-de-lis on it. Originally there were a lot of them scattered about the flag but in 1365 Charles V decreed there should only be three in honour of the Blessed Trinity. Until 1802 the Kings of England claimed to be Kings of France as well, which is why the French fleurs-de-lis on a blue background are seen in the arms of nearly all the British Kings up to and including George III.

A curious optical illusion occurs: if the stripes of the tricolour are all the same width, the red stripe looks narrower than the others. In order to make the stripes *appear* the same width, the proportions are: blue 33 per cent, white 30 per cent and red 37 per cent.

GABON

A small west African country, which used to belong to France. Its flag is a horizontal tricolour, green over yellow over blue.

GAMBIA

Another small country in west Africa. It formerly belonged to Britain. When it became independent in 1965 it adopted a horizontal tricolour of red over blue over green with narrow white stripes on the upper and lower edges of the blue part.

GERMANY

Germany has two flags, one for West Germany – the West German Federal Republic – a plain horizontal tricolour of black over red over yellow. The other is for East Germany – the East German Democratic Republic. This uses the same flag with the addition, in the centre, of a wreath surrounding a pair of yellow dividers in front of a hammer of the same colour.

From 1867 until the end of the First World War the German flag was a horizontal tricolour of black over white over red. This is a combination of the flag of Prussia, which was black and white, and the flag of the Hanseatic League, a group of mercantile trading cities in North Germany, whose flag was red and white.

When Hitler was in power Germany adopted a red flag with a white circle in the middle. On this was placed a symbol called a fylfot, or swastika.

GHANA

Formerly the Gold Coast, a British possession in west Africa. It became independent in 1957 and took as its flag a horizontal tricolour of red over yellow over green with a black star in the centre.

GIBRALTAR

This is a rocky promontory belonging to Britain on the south coast of Spain, at the western end of the Mediterranean Sea. Its flag is the Blue Ensign with Gibraltar's badge in the fly. This is a white roundel on which is an unusually shaped red shield which has a triple-towered grey castle on it. Hanging below the castle entrance is a gold key.

GILBERT ISLANDS

This group of islands in the Pacific is a British dependent territory. They fly the Blue Ensign with a shield in the fly. This is mainly red. At the bottom are some blue and white wavy lines representing the sea out of which a golden sun is rising. In the top of the shield a gold frigate bird is flying.

GREAT BRITAIN

The national flag of Great Britain is the Union Jack. See p. 30.

GREECE

Greece is one of the oldest countries in civilization. It is in southeast Europe bordering Turkey and Asia. It has two flags, one normally used only *inside* the country and one for use *outside* the country – on the sea, or flying over its embassies in foreign lands.

The flag used inside Greece is pale blue with a white St George's cross on it. The other flag has a white St George's cross on royal blue in the canton with the rest of the flag having five blue and four white stripes. There is a tradition that these nine stripes represent the nine syllables in the motto of Greece, '*Eleutheria i thanatos*', which means 'Liberty or death'.

GREENLAND

Greenland is ruled by Denmark and uses that country's flag (see p. 71).

GRENADA

Grenada is one of the Windward group of islands. It has a green and yellow flag with a red border which has six five-pointed yellow stars on it. At the centre of the flag is a red roundel on which is another five-pointed yellow star. On the green part of the flag in the hoist is a nutmeg. The green represents the island's agriculture, the yellow is an emblem of the friendliness of the people and the red symbolizes harmony. The seven stars represent the seven parishes or administrative districts of the island and the nutmeg is Grenada's principal product.

GUATEMALA

Formerly a member of the United Provinces of Central America with El Salvador and Honduras, its flag is a vertical tricolour of blue, white and blue. On the central white part is the country's emblem, which is rather complicated. Basically it comprises a wreath of leaves, two crossed rifles, a colourful bird and a parchment scroll bearing the words '*Libertad 15 de Septiembre 1821*' (Liberty 15 September 1821) which was the date Guatemala gained its independence from Spain.

GUINEA

Guinea is on the west coast of Africa. It has a vertical tricolour of red then yellow then green stripes; very like the flag of its neighbour Mali, the colours of which are the other way round. You have to look carefully to see which is which as it is very easy to confuse them.

GUINEA BISSAU

Guinea Bissau once belonged to Portugal. Its flag is half yellow and half green in the fly, with a red hoist on which is a five-pointed black star. This flag is very similar to the Cape Verde Islands flag.

GUYANA

Guyana in South America was a British Colony – called British Guiana – until it was granted independence within the Commonwealth in 1966. Its flag is rather unusual. It is green with two triangles extending from the flag-pole side (the hoist), a large yellow one with a narrow white edging and on it a smaller dusky brown one with black edging.

HAITI

The western half of the island of San Domingo or Hispaniola, in the Caribbean, of which the Dominican Republic forms the eastern half. Haiti used to be under French rule but in 1804 the coloured inhabitants rose in revolt and gained their independence. To show they were free of white domination they tore the central white stripe from the French tricolour and made their flag from the remaining blue and red parts. This blue and red flag was retained by Haiti until 1968 when it was changed to black and red.

HOLLAND

Holland's flag is probably the oldest of all tricolours. The stripes are horizontal, red over white over blue. It was first used in the 1590s when the Dutch, under their leader the Prince of Orange, rebelled against their Spanish rulers. Originally the colours were orange over white over blue. Red was later substituted for orange because it is easier to distinguish at sea.

HONDURAS

Like El Salvador and Guatemala, Honduras formerly belonged to the United Provinces of Central America. Like the other two it retains the Federation's colours of blue and white in its flag, a horizontal tricolour of blue over white over blue with five blue stars on the white part. The stars are said to symbolize Honduras's hope that the five countries which used to form the United Provinces will again be united one day.

HONG KONG

A British possession just off the south coast of China. It flies the Blue Ensign with its coat of arms on a white roundel in the fly. This shows a crowned lion and a Chinese dragon in gold standing on a green island supporting a shield which is white with two junks – Chinese sailing ships – sailing in the sea in the lower part and, in the upper part, red with a gold naval crown. Above the shield is a half lion in gold crowned and holding a pearl between its paws. On a scroll below the shield are the words 'Hong Kong'.

HUNGARY

Hungary's flag is a horizontal tricolour of red over white over green. In the centre it may have the country's arms underneath a red star, surrounded by a wreath. Or it may have an emblem comprising a yellow hammer and an ear of corn under a red star, surrounded by a wreath of corn.

ICELAND

Iceland has a blue flag on which is a red cross with white edging. Like other Scandinavian countries the vertical arm of the cross is placed off centre towards the hoist.

INDIA

When India gained its independence from Britain in 1947 it adopted an orange over white over green horizontal tricolour. On the central white stripe is a very ancient emblem called the *Chakra*, which means the 'Wheel of Law' and symbolizes orderly change.

INDONESIA

A group of between 3,000 and 4,000 islands in south-east Asia. It used to be known as the Dutch East Indies. When it gained its independence from Holland in 1949 it adopted a horizontally divided flag of red over white. This is very like Poland's flag (see p. 92) which is white over red.

IRAN

A kingdom of west Asia which is ruled over by the Shah; it used to be called Persia. It is an important oil-producing country which has close and friendly links with Britain. Its flag is a horizontal tricolour of green over white over red. This flag is particularly distinctive because it is three times as long as it is broad.

IRAQ

Iraq, which lies between the Euphrates and the Tigris rivers, used to be called Mesopotamia. Its flag, a horizontal tricolour of red over white over black, has three green stars on the white stripe.

IRELAND (Republic of Ireland, Eire)

When Ireland became independent in 1921 it adopted a vertical tricolour of green, white and yellow. Green has always been the colour of Ireland, which is sometimes called the Emerald Isle. It is also a very Catholic country so to its green it added the Vatican colours of white and yellow. However after only a very short while it changed the yellow to orange to commemorate Ulster, Ireland's northern province, which supported William III, Prince of Orange, when he became king instead of James II.

ISLE OF MAN

The Isle of Man has a red flag with three legs in white and gold armour bent at the knee and conjoined at the thigh. It is called the 'Triacria' and is thought to be based on an old Sicilian emblem.

ISRAEL

Israel used to be called Palestine, until it became an independent country in 1948. Its flag is white with two narrow blue horizontal stripes, one just below the upper and the other just above the lower edge. In the centre are two interlaced triangles forming a star which is known throughout the world as the Star of David. David, whose story is told in the Bible, was a famous Jewish king, who ruled about 3,000 years ago.

ITALY

Italy was for a long time a collection of small states: Piedmont, Sardinia, Modena, the Papal States and so on. In 1806 Napoleon made himself King of Italy and gave the country a tricolour like that of France but with a green stripe instead of a blue one. Although the flag went out of use after Napoleon's defeat it was revived in 1870, with the addition of the arms of the House of Savoy in the centre, but in 1946 Italy became a republic and reverted to the plain flag devised for it by Napoleon.

JAMAICA

A Caribbean island, which once belonged to Britain. In 1962, when it became independent, it adopted a new and distinctive flag. This has a yellow St Andrew's cross on a background which is green at the top and bottom and black at the sides.

JAPAN

In Japanese the name for Japan is 'Nippon' which means 'the source of the sun'. The country's flag commemorates this symbolically. The national flag is very simple: it is white with a large plain red circular disc on it representing the sun.

JORDAN

This kingdom in the Middle East once belonged to Turkey. Its flag is a horizontal tricolour, black over white over green with, in the hoist, a red triangle on which is a single white star.

KAMPUCHEA

In south-east Asia. In January 1976 it adopted a new flag which is red with a representation of the temple at Angkor Vat in yellow in the centre. Until recently Kampuchea was called Cambodia.

KENYA

A former British Colony in east Africa. When it became independent in 1963 it adopted a horizontal tricolour of black over red over green with a narrow white stripe on the upper and lower edges of the red stripe. In the centre of the flag is a long oval African shield in front of two crossed spears called 'assegais'.

KOREA

Korea is in Asia. Until 1945 Korea was ruled by Japan. Like Germany it is split into two parts, North Korea, which is under Communist control, and South Korea.

The flag of North Korea has a blue background and a white-edged broad red horizontal stripe on which is a white circle with a red star in the middle of it.

The South Korean flag is white with a red and blue circular

disc, divided in the middle by a wavy line, called a *yin-yang*. In each corner of the flag are some short black diagonal lines. The disc and the black lines are symbols used in Confucianism, the principal Korean religion. The disc, representing light and dark, symbolizes the complementary forces of nature. The lines, called trigrams, have many meanings. On the flag they symbolize the four elements: ☰ air, ☲ fire, ☷ earth, ☵ water.

KUWAIT

A small Middle Eastern oil-producing country. Its flag is a horizontal tricolour of green over white over red. In the hoist is a black triangle with the point cut off (this shape, or geometrical figure, is called a trapezium).

LAOS

Laos is in south-east Asia. Since December 1975 its flag has been blue with a white disc between two horizontal red stripes.

LEBANON

Lebanon, on the eastern shores of the Mediterranean, used to belong to France. Its flag is a horizontal tricolour, red over white over red; in the centre is a cedar tree representing the famous 'Cedars of Lebanon'.

LESOTHO

Formerly a British Protectorate in south Africa. It used to be called Basutoland until 1966, when it became independent. It has a blue flag with a native hat on it in white. In the hoist is a vertically divided red and green stripe.

LIBERIA

Liberia, in west Africa, became independent in 1847. It was originally founded in 1822 as a home for the freed American Negro slaves. Because of the country's connection with America its flag is very similar. It has six red and five white horizontal stripes and a blue canton with just one star on it. The eleven stripes are traditionally believed to symbolize the eleven men who signed Liberia's declaration of independence.

LIBYA

An oil-producing country in north Africa. Its flag is almost exactly the same as Egypt's. It is a horizontal tricolour red over white over black with a yellow eagle emblem in the centre. The only difference between this flag and Egypt's is that the Arabic wording on the scroll beneath the eagle reads 'Arab Republic of Libya'.

LIECHTENSTEIN

On the borders of Austria and Switzerland, it is one of the smallest countries in the world. It is a principality and has a horizontally divided flag, blue over red, with a prince's crown, in gold, in the canton.

LUXEMBOURG

Once closely connected administratively with Holland, it used the same flag as the Dutch until 1890, when it changed the colour of the bottom stripe to light blue. So now it has a horizontal tricolour of red over white over light blue.

MALAGASY REPUBLIC

This is an island, formerly called Madagascar, which lies near Africa in the Indian Ocean. Until recently it belonged to France. Its flag has a white stripe in the hoist and the fly is divided horizontally red over green.

MALAWI

A country in east Africa. It once belonged to Britain, when it was called Nyasaland. When it became independent in 1964 it adopted a horizontal tricolour of black over red over green. On the black stripe the rising sun and its rays are symbolized in red.

MALAYSIA

Malaysia is a federation of thirteen states in south-east Asia. When the federation was formed in 1963 it adopted a flag which is rather similar to that of the USA: it has fourteen horizontal stripes, red and white alternately, with a blue canton on which are a yellow crescent moon and a star with fourteen points. The fourteen stripes and the fourteen points of the star symbolized the fourteen states which, at the time, formed the federation. In 1965 one of the states, Singapore, left the federation but the flag remains unchanged.

MALDIVE ISLANDS

This group of islands in the Indian Ocean became independent from Britain in 1965. Its flag is red with a green rectangle in the centre; on the rectangle is a white crescent.

MALI

Mali is in western Africa and used to be called French Sudan. It gained independence from France in 1960 when it adopted both its new name and a new flag. Today the flag is a plain vertical tricolour of green, yellow and red stripes. At first there was a black figure symbolizing a native dancer on the yellow stripe but now this is left out.

MALTA GC

This little island in the Mediterranean has a very long history. In 1974 it became an independent republic. Its flag is divided vertically, white in the hoist and red in the fly. These are the colours of the Sovereign Military Order of Malta (see p. 48) which used to govern the island. During the Second World War the island, which then belonged to Britain, was awarded the George Cross for its courage. This decoration is represented with a narrow red border in the canton.

MAURITANIA

Once part of French West Africa, it became independent in 1960. Its flag is green. In the centre is a yellow star above a crescent.

MAURITIUS

An island in the Indian Ocean. It once belonged to Britain and became independent in 1968. Its flag comprises four horizontal stripes, red over blue over yellow over green.

MEXICO

Mexico is in Central America where the Aztecs used to live. Its flag is a vertical tricolour of green, white and red stripes with the country's emblem in the centre. This emblem is an eagle standing on a cactus plant holding a snake in its beak. It symbolizes an old legend in which the Aztecs were told that they should build their capital where they saw an eagle standing on a cactus plant. One day they did see this and it is there that they built the beginnings of what is now Mexico City.

MONACO

Monaco is a very small country on the south coast of France. Its capital is Monte Carlo. The flag is the same as Indonesia's, namely a horizontally divided one showing red over white. The symbolism is rather different, though. In the Indonesian flag the colours symbolize those of the Indonesian freedom fighters; in Monaco's they are the colours of Monaco's princely ruling family, the Grimaldis.

MONGOLIA

A 'people's republic' in central Asia, lying roughly between China and Russia. Its flag is a vertical tricolour of red, blue and red. On the red stripe nearest the flag pole is an ancient symbol of the country's religion called a '*soyonbo*'. This is coloured yellow and includes the *yin-yang* disc which, in different colours, is also found in the flag of South Korea.

MONTSERRAT

One of the Windward Isles. It is a dependent territory of Britain and flies the Blue Ensign with a shield on a white roundel in the fly. The shield is mainly blue with a sand-coloured base. Standing on the base is a woman dressed in green embracing a black cross with her right arm and resting her left arm on a brown harp.

MOROCCO

Morocco is a country in north Africa. It has a red flag with a rather interesting green five-pointed star in the centre. It is a religious symbol, called a pentagram, formed by interlaced lines.

MOZAMBIQUE

In south-east Africa. It belonged to Portugal until it gained its independence in 1975. The flag which it adopted is unusually distinctive. The upper part is green and the lower part yellow. On a broad stripe starting from the bottom right and narrowing to a point at the top left-hand corner of the flag are two similar stripes: a red one starting from the lower part of the fly and a black one starting from the right-hand end of the bottom of the flag. The black and red stripes are separated by narrow tapering white stripes. Spread over the upper end of the stripes is a white cog-wheel outlined in black. In the centre of the cog-wheel is an open book which is also white and outlined in black. In front of the book is a black sub-machine-gun with a fixed bayonet and a black hoe crossing over each other in St Andrew's Cross form. The point where they actually cross is a little above the book. Just above the right-hand side of the book is a five-pointed red star.

NEPAL

This country, high in the Himalayan mountains to the north-east of India near Tibet, has a most unusual flag. It consists of two right-angled triangles one above the other, both red with blue edging. On the upper one is an emblem symbolizing the moon, and on the lower one an emblem symbolizing the sun. Both emblems are in white.

NETHERLANDS ANTILLES

These are islands in the West Indies. Their flag is white with a cross like the St George's cross but only the vertical part is red. The horizontal arm is blue with six five-pointed white stars on it.

NEW ZEALAND

New Zealand's flag is very similar to that of Australia. It is blue with the Union Jack in the canton and four stars in the fly, again representing the constellation of the Southern Cross. But the stars are red with a white edging instead of all white as in the Australian flag. New Zealand does not have the big Commonwealth Star which the Australian flag shows beneath the Union Jack.

NICARAGUA

Like most of the other small countries in Central America, Nicaragua's flag is predominantly blue and white. It is a horizontal tricolour blue over white over blue. In the centre is the country's emblem – a triangle showing a landscape with five mountains rising out of the sea. On the top of the middle mountain is a pole carrying a red Phrygian cap and between the two right-hand mountains is the rising sun.

NIGER

Another of the former colonies in French West Africa which gained independence in 1960. Its flag is a horizontal tricolour of orange over white over green with a small orange disc in the middle of the central white stripe.

NIGERIA

Nigeria is in west Africa; it became independent from Britain in 1960. Its flag is a vertical tricolour of green, white and green.

NORWAY

Norway was ruled by Denmark from 1397 to 1814, and its flag reflects this as they are very similar. Norway's flag is red with a white edged blue cross. The vertical arm of the cross, as in the flags of the other Scandinavian countries, is slightly off centre towards the hoist.

OMAN

A small Arab state at the eastern end of the Persian Gulf. For many centuries its flag was plain red. It adopted its present one in 1970. This has a red hoist and a horizontal tricolour fly. The colours in the fly are white over red over green. The central red stripe is only half the width of the other two stripes. In the top part of the hoist is Oman's national emblem outlined in white. This comprises two Arab swords crossed St Andrew's fashion behind an upright curved Arab dagger, in front of which are the central links of an ornate belt. The white and green stripes in the fly are of religious significance. The white is associated with the Imam, the religious leader of Oman, while green is the sacred colour of Islam.

PAKISTAN

At one time Pakistan was part of India, but when India became independent in 1947, the Muslim part of it became a separate country called Pakistan. Its flag has a white stripe in the hoist, the fly is green with a white crescent moon and a white star.

PANAMA

Panama was part of the Republic of Colombia in Central America until 1903. Its flag is divided into four squares, a white one in the top part of the hoist with a blue star on it, a white one in the lower part of the fly with a red star on it, a blue square in the lower part of the hoist and a red square in the top of the fly.

PAPUA AND NEW GUINEA

These form an island in the south-west Pacific just north of Australia. It was under Australia's control until September 1975, when it became independent. Its flag is divided diagonally from top left to bottom right. The upper half is red and has a yellow bird of paradise on it. The lower half is black with four large and one small white five-pointed stars. These represent the constellation of the Southern Cross.

PARAGUAY

A small country in South America. Its flag is like Holland's, a horizontal tricolour of red over white over dark blue. On one side of the flag the middle stripe has a badge with a star in it. In the same place on the other side is a lion and a Phrygian cap, which is a revolutionary symbol.

PERU

One of the larger countries of South America. It has a vertical tricolour of red, white and red stripes; on the white central stripe is Peru's coat of arms. There is an old tradition that the red and white colours are taken from the plumage of some birds which were seen as the Peruvian freedom fighters first started their fight for independence.

PHILIPPINE ISLANDS

The Philippine Islands are in south-east Asia; they have been ruled by both Spain and the USA, and became independent in 1946. The flag is the one that was used during the nation's fight against the Spanish in 1894. It is horizontally divided with blue over red and on a white triangle in the hoist is a symbol for the sun between three stars which are coloured yellow.

POLAND

Poland is in north central Europe. Like the Philippines it has been under the rule of other countries for long parts of its history. At the moment it is governed by the Communists. Its flag is divided horizontally white over red, the colours of the old royal arms of Poland, which consisted of a red shield with a white eagle on it.

PORTUGAL

The flag of Portugal is vertically divided with green in the hoist and red in the fly. The green part is rather narrower than the red. Where the two colours join there is a yellow armillary sphere – a skeleton globe – in front of which is the old royal coat of arms of the Braganza family, which used to reign over Portugal. In 1910 the king was murdered, and since then the country has been a republic.

PUERTO RICO

Although under the control of the USA, Puerto Rico is to a large extent self-governing and flies its own flag. This is similar to the Stars and Stripes. It is red with two white stripes, and on a blue triangle in the hoist is one white star. This flag is almost the same as Cuba's but the colours are in a different order.

QUATAR

A small but wealthy oil-producing sheikhdom in south-west Asia. Its flag is similar to that of Bahrein. It has a white stripe in the hoist with a serrated edge separating it from the fly, which is maroon. Quatar's flag is narrower than most national flags.

RHODESIA

Rhodesia declared itself independent of Britain in 1965. The flag it has used since 1968 is a vertical tricolour of green, white and green stripes. On the central white stripe is the country's coat of arms.

ROMANIA

Romania is in the Balkan peninsula in south-east Europe. Its flag used to be a plain vertical tricolour of blue, yellow and red stripes. Since the Communists gained control in 1947 an emblem depicting an oil-well, trees, a mountain valley and a red star has been added to the central stripe.

RUSSIA *see* USSR, p. 102.

RWANDA

Sometimes spelt Ruanda, this is another small central African country which recently (1962) gained its independence. Its flag is a vertical tricolour of red, yellow and green stripes, with a large black R on the centre stripe.

ST HELENA

St Helena is a dependency of Britain. It is an island in the south Atlantic to the west of Africa. The flag is the Blue Ensign with the island's shield in the fly. The shield has a blue background and shows on a green sea a three-masted sailing ship flying the St George's flag and sailing towards two large conical rocks.

ST KITTS-NEVIS

The flag of St Kitts-Nevis, one of the Leeward Islands in the West Indies, is a vertical tricolour, the part nearest the hoist is green, the centre yellow and the fly blue. On the middle of the yellow part is a palm tree. The flag represents the island, showing the green land, a golden beach with palm trees, and the blue seas.

ST LUCIA

An island in the Windward group. Since 1967 its flag has been blue with, in the centre, a white-edged black triangle on which, at the base, is a smaller yellow triangle.

ST VINCENT

Another island in the Windward group. It flies a blue flag with the island's arms in the centre. On the shield are two women at an altar. The crest is a white flower while on the scroll below the shield is the motto '*Pax et Justitia*', which means 'Peace and Justice'.

SAN MARINO

Near Rimini, in eastern Italy, this is a tiny republic which has been independent since the fourth century. Its flag is divided horizontally, the top half being white and the bottom blue. In the centre is its coat of arms showing three peaks of Mount Titano, each topped with a tower capped with an ostrich feather, and with some leaves on each side. Below is the motto '*Libertas*' (Liberty).

SAO TOME E PRINCIPE

A group of islands off the west coast of Africa. They used to belong to Portugal and became independent in 1975. Their flag is a horizontal tricolour of green over yellow over green with a red triangle in the hoist. On the central yellow stripe are two black five-pointed stars.

SAUDI ARABIA

The national flag of Saudi Arabia, a Mohammedan country, has a green field, the Mohammedan sacred colour. On it are white Arabic characters meaning: 'There is no God but Allah, and Mohammed is his prophet'. Below the writing is a white sword with its point towards the hoist.

SENEGAL

A west African country whose flag resembles those of the neighbouring countries of Mali and Guinea, being divided into three vertical stripes, that nearest the hoist green, then yellow, then red. The yellow stripe has a green star in the centre.

SEYCHELLES

The Seychelles are a group of islands in the middle of the Indian Ocean. In 1976 they became independent of Great Britain and took a new flag. This is very similar to Scotland's, having a white St Andrew's cross on a background which is blue at the top and bottom and red at the sides.

SIERRA LEONE

Sierra Leone is in western Africa. Its flag is a horizontal tricolour of green over white over blue.

SIKKIM

A small country lying between Tibet and India, it is independent but protected by India. Its flag is white with a red border, and in the centre of the flag is a red and gold wheel.

SINGAPORE

An independent island off the Malay coast. When it withdrew from the Federation of Malaysia in 1965 it kept its former flag, which is horizontally halved with red at the top and white at the base. In the hoist on the red half is a crescent moon and five stars in white. The stars represent Justice, Democracy, Peace, Equality and Progress.

SOLOMON ISLANDS

These are a dependency of Britain and are in the Pacific Ocean. Their flag is the Blue Ensign showing their coat of arms on a white roundel in the fly. This is quartered blue and white showing respectively an eagle, a turtle, some native weapons and two frigate birds. The top of the shield is red with a gold lion on it.

SOMALIA

Somalia is now an independent country on the east coast of Africa, made up of the former two colonies of Italian and British Somaliland. The flag is sky blue with a white star in the centre.

SOUTH AFRICA

Formed of four colonies settled by the Dutch (Boers) in Natal, the Orange Free State and the Transvaal and the British in Cape Colony. After the Boer War (1899–1902) the four regions were united as one country in the British Empire. The present flag, which clearly shows the history of the country, was adopted when it gained dominion status in 1926, and retained when South Africa left the Commonwealth to become independent in 1961. The flag is a horizontal tricolour of orange at the top, then white, then blue. In the centre of the white stripe and nearest to the hoist is the Union Jack, in the centre is the flag of the Orange Free State – four orange and three white stripes, with, in its top left-hand corner, the tricolour flag of the Netherlands. The third small flag on the right is that of the Transvaal, the modern Dutch flag, but with a green vertical stripe in the hoist.

SPAIN

Spain's national flag is a tricolour of three horizontal stripes, red over yellow over red – the colours of the House of Aragon. In the hoist are the arms of Spain. It is said that the red and yellow colours of Spain date from the Middle Ages, when, after a battle, one of the kings of Aragon – part of Spain – dipped two of his fingers in some blood and then drew one across the top and one across the bottom of his yellow shield.

SRI LANKA

Sri Lanka was known as Ceylon until it became independent in 1948. It adopted the old flag of the Kings of Kandy – formerly part of Ceylon – which was crimson with a yellow lion holding an upright sword. Since then two vertical bars of green and orange have been added in the hoist, to represent the other peoples of Ceylon. Around the edge of the flag and dividing the hoist from the fly is a yellow edging.

SUDAN

Sudan is the largest country in Africa; it lies south of Egypt, and has been ruled by Egypt at various periods of its history. From 1899 it was ruled jointly by Egypt and Britain; in 1956 it became independent. Its flag is a tricolour of three horizontal stripes, red over white over black, with a green triangle in the hoist.

SURINAM

Surinam, once called Dutch Guinea, is a country in the northern part of South America. It has a striking flag of five horizontal stripes. Green over white over red over white over green. The central red stripe is twice as wide as the green stripes, which are twice as wide as the white stripes. It has a five-pointed gold star in the centre.

SWAZILAND

Swaziland was a British Protectorate in south Africa until it became an independent kingdom in 1968. The flag consists of two horizontal blue stripes separated by a wider red stripe edged with yellow. On the red stripe across the middle of the flag is a native shield of black and white in front of two spears and a staff. The shield and staff have blue tassels on them.

SWEDEN

Sweden's flag has a gold cross on a blue background, the colours of the Swedish royal family. The flag was first used when Sweden became independent of Denmark in 1523, and re-adopted when it left the Union of Sweden and Norway in 1905. The other Scandinavian countries have rather similar flags using a cross, and, like them, the vertical stripe of the cross lies off centre towards the hoist.

SWITZERLAND

A very mountainous country in central Europe, which finally became independent of Austrian rule in 1648. The legendary William Tell was one of the heroes who fought for the country's freedom. The flag consists of a small white cross on a red background. The Red Cross Organization (see p. 48) was started by a Swiss national, Jean Henri Dunant, in 1859, and has its head-quarters in Geneva, a large city in western Switzerland.

SYRIA

Syria is Arab country in western Africa. Its flag is almost identical to that of Egypt and Libya. It is a horizontal tricolour of red over white over black with a golden eagle emblem above a scroll bearing in Arabic script the words 'Arab Republic of Syria'.

TANZANIA

An independent country in eastern Africa formed from two separate countries, Tanganyika and Zanzibar. They were under German rule until the end of the First World War, when they became British. They were given their independence in 1961 and 1963 respectively, and in 1964 joined together to become the United Republic of Tanzania. The flag consists of a wide black stripe with narrow yellow edges running from bottom left to top right. The fly side of the stripe is blue and the hoist side green.

THAILAND

Thailand, formerly called Siam, is an ancient kingdom in south-east Asia. Its flag has a broad blue horizontal stripe edged above and below by a narrower stripe of white, with further stripes of red bordering the top and bottom of the flag. Thailand, sometimes called 'The Land of the White Elephant', once used a red flag with a white elephant in the centre.

TIBET

Since being taken over by China in 1950 Tibet has used the Communist Chinese flag. Before that time it had its own flag. This was rather ornate, having a narrow yellow border along the top, hoist and bottom sides, and the sun rising from behind a white triangle at the base (representing a mountain), with alternate blue and red rays. On the triangle, below a jewel, was a pearl between two lions.

TOGO

Togo is in western Africa and was formerly under French rule. It has for its flag five vertical stripes, three of green and two of yellow, with a white star on a red canton.

TONGA

Tonga is a little group of islands in the Pacific Ocean just north of New Zealand. Its flag is red with a white canton and on the canton is a red cross. The red symbolizes the blood shed by Christ and the cross in the canton commemorates the cross on which he died. Tonga has flown this flag since 1875.

TRINIDAD AND TOBAGO

Trinidad and Tobago are two islands in the West Indies. They became independent of Britain in 1962, and adopted a red flag with a black stripe edged on both sides with white, running from top left to bottom right. The asphalt used to surface our roads comes from a lake in Trinidad.

TUNISIA

Tunisia is in north Africa. It was formerly a French Protectorate. Many of its people are Mohammedans. Its flag is red with a white circle in the middle on which are a red crescent and star.

TURKEY

Turkey, which straddles Europe and Asia, is one of the largest of the Mohammedan countries. The crescent moon and star which appear in white on Turkey's red flag were the symbols of the great Ottoman Empire of which Turkey was a part.

TURKS AND CAICOS ISLANDS

These islands are in the West Indies; they are a British dependency. Their flag is the Blue Ensign with a shield in the fly. The shield is yellow, with a conch shell, a spiny lobster and a Turk's head cactus on it in their natural colours.

TUVALU

Tuvalu is a group of islands in the western Pacific. They are a British dependency and until recently were known as the Ellice Islands. Tuvalu flies the Blue Ensign with its coat of arms in a white roundel in the fly. (Not illustrated.)

UGANDA

Uganda is in eastern Africa. Its flag has six horizontal stripes which, starting from the top, are coloured black, yellow, red, black, yellow, red. In the centre, on a white roundel, is a white crested crane, the national bird of Uganda.

UNITED ARAB REPUBLIC

These were formerly known as the Trucial States. Their flag is a horizontal tricolour of green over white over black with a red hoist.

UNITED STATES OF AMERICA

The flag of America is the Stars and Stripes. It has seven red and six white stripes. On the blue canton are fifty white stars, one for every state in the Union. The thirteen coloured stripes represent the thirteen original states of the Union. See p. 37.

UPPER VOLTA

A country in western Africa. It was formerly a French colony. Upper Volta's flag is symbolic of its three main rivers, the black, white and red Voltas, and is divided into three horizontal stripes of black over white over red.

URUGUAY

Uruguay is a small country in eastern South America, between Brazil and the Argentine. Its flag is rather similar to that of Argentina, having nine horizontal stripes, five white and four blue. On a white canton is a sun, which has a face on it, surrounded by sixteen rays.

USSR

The flag of Russia is blood red. In the canton is a yellow sickle crossed by a hammer of the same colour. Above the sickle is a red five-pointed star outlined in yellow.

VATICAN CITY

This is the smallest, but possibly one of the most important states in the world as it is the very heart of Christianity. Its ruler is the Pope. Its flag is divided vertically, yellow and white commemorating the colours of Jerusalem. In the fly are the tiara, or triple crown, which is symbolic of the three crowns worn by the Holy Trinity conjoined in the singleness of God, and the crossed keys of St Peter. These are sometimes called the Keys of Heaven. One is gold, symbolizing the key which looses, and the other silver, symbolizing the key which binds. It became the official flag in 1809 under Pope Pius VII.

VENEZUELA

Venezuela is in South America. Its flag is similar in colour to those of Ecuador and Colombia, its near neighbours, but the width of its stripes is equal. It is a horizontal tricolour, yellow over blue over red. On the blue stripe is a semicircle of seven white stars. In the canton is the country's badge.

VIETNAM

Vietnam is in south-east Asia. Its flag is blood red with a five-pointed yellow star in the centre. The colour represents the ruthlessness and the star the godlessness of its new masters, the communists.

WESTERN SAMOA

In the Pacific Ocean, ruled, until 1962, from New Zealand. When it became independent it adopted a red flag with four large and one small five-pointed stars, representing the constellation of the Southern Cross on a blue canton.

YEMEN ARAB REPUBLIC

A country in the Arabian peninsula. Its flag is a horizontal tri-colour of red over white over black with one green star in the centre.

YEMEN (People's Democratic Republic of)

Formerly South Arabia until it became independent of Britain in 1967. Its flag is a tricolour of horizontal stripes, red over white over black, with a red star on the blue triangle in the hoist.

YUGOSLAVIA

Yugoslavia is in south-east Europe. It was formed after the First World War from part of the Austro–Hungarian Empire and some independent states. Its flag is a horizontal tricolour, blue over white over red. In the centre is a large yellow-edged red star. The red, white and blue symbolize two of the principal countries which form Yugoslavia, namely Serbia and Montenegro, while the red star denotes that it has a Communist government.

ZAIRE

The former Belgian Congo is now called Zaire and has its capital at Kinshasa. Its flag is green. In the middle is a red-edged yellow roundel on which is a chocolate-coloured forearm holding a flaming torch.

ZAMBIA

Zambia used to be called Northern Rhodesia. It became independent in 1964. Its flag is particularly distinctive because it is rather unusual. It is mainly green but in the lower part of the fly is a vertical tricolour of red, black and orange stripes above which is an orange eagle with its wings outstretched.

Index

HEARD ABOUT THE PUFFIN CLUB?

... it's a way of finding out more about Puffin Books
and authors, of winning prizes (in competitions),
sharing jokes, a secret code, and perhaps seeing your
name in print! When you join you get a copy of our
magazine, *Puffin Post*, sent to you four times a year,
a badge and a membership book.

For details of subscription and an application form,
send a stamped addressed envelope to:

The Puffin Club Dept A
Penguin Books Limited
Bath Road
Harmondsworth
Middlesex UB7 ODA

and if you live in Australia, please write to:

The Australian Puffin Club
Penguin Books Australia Limited
P.O. Box 257
Ringwood
Victoria 3134